T0358543

Farming and Food Supplies

In the 1960s, the farming industry of Britain had been transformed and modernised to the point where output per person was the highest in Europe. Many farmers reasoned from this that there should be expansion of agriculture rather than restriction, and that the natural resources of Britain should be developed to the full. Originally published in 1965, this book examines the case for further expansion against the background of mass hunger and rising population in many parts of the world. The case rests upon three premises. The first is that the farming industry is now making an indispensable contribution to the national economy. The second is that the industry is capable of further development in output and efficiency. The third is that there is likely to be a scarcity of food on the world markets over the next twenty to thirty years rather than a surplus.

Margaret Bramley believed that the final choice of policy should be based upon the long-term interests of the whole community, not upon the sectional interests of farmers, food importers or distributors. She said it was essential to recall how vulnerable as a small densely populated island Britain is, with half our food at the time coming from overseas.

With recent world events bringing the subject of food distribution to the fore, the book's advocacy of expansion of British farming resonates strongly again today.

Farming and Food Supplies

The Case for Expansion of British Agriculture

Margaret Bramley

First published in 1965
by George Allen & Unwin Ltd

This edition first published in 2024 by Routledge
4 Park Square, Milton Park, Abingdon, Oxon, OX14 4RN

and by Routledge
605 Third Avenue, New York, NY 10017

Routledge is an imprint of the Taylor & Francis Group, an informa business

Publisher's Note
The publisher has gone to great lengths to ensure the quality of this reprint but points out that some imperfections in the original copies may be apparent.

Disclaimer
The publisher has made every effort to trace copyright holders and welcomes correspondence from those they have been unable to contact.

A Library of Congress record exists under LCCN: 65029607

ISBN: 978-1-032-81888-7 (hbk)
ISBN: 978-1-003-50191-6 (ebk)
ISBN: 978-1-032-81897-9 (pbk)

Book DOI 10.4324/9781003501916

FARMING
AND
FOOD SUPPLIES

THE CASE FOR EXPANSION
OF BRITISH AGRICULTURE

BY

MARGARET BRAMLEY

London

GEORGE ALLEN & UNWIN LTD

RUSKIN HOUSE · MUSEUM STREET

FIRST PUBLISHED IN 1965

PRINTED IN GREAT BRITAIN
in 10 on 11 point Pilgrim type
BY EAST MIDLAND PRINTING CO. LTD.
BURY ST. EDMUNDS

FOREWORD

IF we were fortunate enough to have a static world population, the task of raising nutritional standards to an adequate level would be enormous. It would require a huge investment in agricultural education, in land development and engineering works, and in the chemical industries on which modern farming depends. The problem, however, is much more complex, for the expectation is that by the time our teen-age Beatle fans have reached middle-age respectability there will be 6,000,000,000 mouths to feed, or twice as many as there are today. There is no time for delay or manoeuvre because every year seems to bring a reminder of what is in store – for instance, crop failures in Russia and China, and famine in India.

Every acre of cultivatable land will become important and every useful technical advance will have to be exploited if we are to meet the challenge of the next thirty years. Unfortunately current thinking does not appear to take cognizance of the task or the enormity of the effort that has to be made. The threat of atomic warfare stimulates protest marches and demonstrations, but international goodwill and common-sense can avert the catastrophe of the bomb. It will require careful planning and hard work as well to avert an even greater tragedy of chronic famine and malnutrition for millions in the underdeveloped countries.

Mrs Bramley's book gives a thoughtful and balanced assessment of the situation and underlines the urgency of action. As she points out, we cannot achieve spectacular increases in production at a moment's notice, for there is an inertia due to ignorance, complacency and selfishness that has to be overcome before worthwhile momentum is obtained. We, in Britain, cannot be isolated from this effort. With our limited acres we are in a specially vulnerable position, and it is idle to think that in twenty years' time we will be enjoying a buyer's market for world food surpluses. We just cannot live in the past, for the simple fact is that the level of nutrition of this country is going to depend more and more on what we produce from our own land. The comforting thought is that even with existing knowledge there is an enormous production potential that can be realized.

I sincerely hope that this book will be read widely and that it will stimulate critical thought, especially in high places where decisions are taken about the use of land. I hope, too, that it will be read by the leaders of the farming industry so that they will be concerned less with the immediate present and Price Review wrangles and more with the long term developments of British agriculture. It should be compulsory reading for every school-leaver, for it is this rising generation who will be meeting the problems that will face civilization at the turn of the century.

M. M. Cooper

ACKNOWLEDGEMENTS

The work on this book would not have been possible without the excellent service of the NFU Postal Library, and my grateful thanks are due to the librarians for their expert help and for their unfailing patience in waiting for overdue books and reports to be returned. I should also like to thank the NFU Information Department for advice on some of the statistics.

Finally, I would like to express my deep appreciation to the Sir Halley Stewart Trust for their generosity in making a contribution towards the cost of publishing this book.

Margaret Bramley
Little Trees Farm
Kinsbourne Green
Herts
March 1965

CONTENTS

INTRODUCTION

THE icy winter of 1963 marked a turning point for British farming. In the midst of snow blizzards, fierce gales and savage frosts, farmers struggled to save their livelihood from disaster, to rescue sheep and cattle, to keep milk supplies moving, under the worst conditions ever known. Against this grim and sombre background, the abrupt ending of the Common Market negotiations compelled a new assessment of farming policy.

Over several years, farmers had been restive under the pressure of rising costs and declining farm incomes, whilst Parliament had been uneasy at the rising bill for subsidies. It was clear that some changes in policy were needed. For a time, it seemed likely that British farming would have to conform to the European system of tariffs and import levies, laid down in Brussels. But once the negotiations ended, it became urgent to work out a new and independent policy for British farming.

The Government has at its disposal many devices for controlling and influencing the farming industry, including grants, subsidies, standard quantities and import controls. But these tools, in themselves, cannot determine the long-term development of farming – it depends how they are used. Certain deeper questions of principle remain unsettled. How does farming rate as part of our economic life? Is it an essential industry, such as coal mining, or an expendable occupation, such as operating bingo halls? Again, is there an abundance of food being produced in other countries, which Britain can buy cheaply in return for industrial exports, or is it likely that in the years to come there will be a world food shortage?

Amongst many city people, farming has a very low rating indeed. In an article on 'The Age of Leisure', an economist, Professor Alan Day, wrote: –

'. . . we insist on devoting our land to farming, when the Commonwealth, the Americans and the Europeans are all falling over themselves to sell us food at lower prices than we can produce it ourselves. The Green Belts should be places where we can take the dog for a walk across open fields rather than places where market gardeners grow tomatoes in greenhouses. We can get food from the remote parts of the country or from abroad, but Londoners cannot picnic in Manitoba or New Zealand."[1]

The implication is that food production in the United Kingdom is of minor importance, and ample food supplies can be obtained from abroad. From this it is a short step to deliberate restriction of agriculture. For instance, Professor Colin Clark wants to cut down drastically the number of people working on the land, and to concentrate the farms into a few large units. He believes that : –

'Production will have to be reduced in certain directions and prevented from rising in others.'[2]

It becomes clear that the doctrine of 'cheap food from abroad', which dominated British thinking for two generations, is still very much alive.

But, in fact, the farming industry has been transformed in the last twenty-five years. It has been modernized and mechanized to the point where output per man is the highest in Europe. Many farmers reason from this that there should be expansion of agriculture rather than restriction, and that the natural resources of Britain should be developed to the full. A choice has to be made between these two opposing policies.

This book examines the case for expansion – a case which rests upon three premises. The first is that the farming industry is now making an indispensable contribution to the national economy. The second is that the industry is capable of further development in output and efficiency. The third is that there is likely to be a scarcity of food on the world markets over the next twenty to thirty years rather than a surplus.

The final choice of policy should be based upon the long-term interests of the whole community, not upon the sectional interests of farmers, food importers or distributors. It is essential to recall how vulnerable is this small densely populated island, with half our food coming from overseas. By the end of the century, it is expected that our population will have increased by twenty millions, and our food requirements will be much greater

---

[1] Prof. Alan Day. *Observer* July 28, 1963.
[2] Prof. Colin Clark. *Journal* of Farmers Club Jan. 10, 1962.

than at present. If, as is possible, the supplies of grain, meat and dairy products on the world markets became scarcer and dearer, our balance of trade would be worsened and our standard of living would be endangered. In a world in which nearly half the people are hungry, Britain, of all countries, cannot afford to be complacent about food supplies.

PART I

FARMING IN THE
NATIONAL ECONOMY

CHAPTER I

FARMING -
A MAJOR INDUSTRY

AGRICULTURE is still the principal occupation of mankind, and in many parts of the world economic prosperity is precariously balanced on the success or failure of the annual harvest. Even in industrialized countries in Western Europe, 20-30% of the population are engaged in farming, and food production is regarded as one of the foundations of economic life. In these countries, home produced food is primary and imported food secondary. Imports are a make-weight – to increase the supply of basic foods, and to supplement the diet with tropical products, such as tea, coffee, oranges and bananas. In Britain, for historical reasons, this outlook has been turned upside down. Imported products, particularly from the Commonwealth, have been looked upon as the main source of food supply, with home agriculture being the make-weight, to provide fresh milk and vegetables, and a few kinds of fruit. Respect for the overseas farmer has been matched by contempt for the British farmer.

This attitude, with the accompanying depression and degradation of the farming industry, arose from the unique position of the British economy during the nineteenth century. As the first country to establish manufacturing industry, Britain had, for a time, a commanding position in world trade. Looking back from 1960, it seems almost incredible that a hundred years ago the United Kingdom was supplying half the world's output of coal and manufactured goods.[1] The opening up of new farm lands in North America, and later in Australia and New Zealand, made possible a plentiful supply of cheap imported food. The acquisition of extensive colonial territories in Africa, the West Indies and the Far East secured further markets, in addition to those

[1] J. H. Dunning & C. J. Thomas. *British Industry*. (Hutchinson 1960.)

already controlled in India. This combination of circumstances brought immense wealth and power to British manufacturers, shipowners and financiers. It was hardly surprising that the gradual destruction of British farming seemed a small price to pay.

For those who lived and worked in the countryside, the price was a bitter one. During the 1930's, farm workers were existing on wages of around 34s per week. Land was being sold for £5 an acre, and landlords were so desperate for tenants that they would let a man have a farm rent-free for three years, and plough it up for him, to get him to take it on. Bankruptcies were a common occurrence, and the farmer had to stand by and see his assets sold up to pay his creditors. But sometimes his neighbours would rally round, and by tacit agreement buy his tackle at knock-out prices at the sale, only to give it back to him a few weeks later!

Prices were so low that land and farms were falling into decay. Lord Addison found :—

'. . . that millions of acres of land have passed out of active cultivation, and that the process is continuing; that an increasing extent of good land is reverting to tufts of inferior grass, to brambles and weeds, and often to the reedy growth that betrays water-logging; that multitudes of farms are beset with dilapidated buildings, and that a great and rapid diminution is taking place in the number who find employment upon them.'[2]

The agricultural depression continued, until in 1938 two-thirds of our food requirements were being imported. Dependence upon imported food was not seen as a strategic danger or an economic weakness by those in authority. They regarded home agriculture as a bargaining counter, to be sacrificed whenever necessary to secure foreign markets for industrial goods. This outlook is not merely of historical interest : it is deeply embedded in British thinking to this day.

But, in reality, Britain's trading position has changed so much that this approach no longer fits the facts. Six years of war against Nazi Germany left Britain impoverished, with export trade disrupted, and large debts outstanding to the United States and other

---

[2] Lord Addison. *A Policy for British Agriculture*, p.14. (Gollancz 1939.)

nations. National Independence Movements in India, Africa and Malaya loosened the close economic ties with Britain, and the emerging Commonwealth countries began to look elsewhere for trade and capital investment. Ironically, the defeated nations – West Germany and Japan – made the most rapid recovery from war damage, and within ten years were surpassing Britain in industrial productivity. Whereas, a generation ago, Britain was second only to the United States in economic and financial power, today there are many strong rivals – Canada, France, West Germany, Italy, Japan and the Soviet Union – keenly competing for world markets. It is now very much harder for Britain to 'earn a living', and pay for essential imports. In recent years, the threat of a balance of payments crisis has never been very far distant.

In this same period, the farming industry has changed out of all recognition. Faced with blockade and possible starvation at the beginning of the war, the Government started an intensive drive to raise food production. This set in motion a revolution in farming methods – in machinery, buildings, plant breeding, crop growing and animal husbandry, and this revolution has continued with increasing momentum ever since. The stability provided by the guaranteed price system encouraged farmers to invest in new developments of all kinds. Whilst there are still wide differences between farm and farm, and between different localities, the overall result has been a very great increase in production. By 1964, it was nearly double the pre-war average. Among the most striking advances have been the increase in the average yield of wheat from 17.8 cwt. per acre pre-war to 29.7 cwt. today, and of sugar beet from 8.2 tons per acre to 14.8 tons per acre. Average milk yields have risen from 540 gallons per cow to 636 gallons, and tuberculosis in cattle has been completely eradicated. Beef production has increased by 54%, and pigmeat and eggs have nearly doubled.[3] As a result of this expansion, home agriculture is now supplying two-thirds of our requirements of temperate foodstuffs (those which can be grown in the British climate) and about half our total food requirements, including tropical products.

Today, the countryside is no longer derelict. Farms are well

---

[3] NFU. 'Britain's Biggest Industry'. 1963.

stocked with first-class machinery, and many new buildings have been erected. Fine crops and thriving cattle can be seen in many counties. Even in the hill country in Wales and Scotland, where conditions are harder, land is being reclaimed from heather and bracken for sheep grazing, and new forests are being planted. On closer examination, the effects of the long era of depression are still to be seen in tumble-down cottages, awkward layouts, and obsolete buildings standing alongside new ones. But instead of decay and despair, there is life and activity.

The output of British farming, in terms of cash, is impressive. The townsman is inclined to think that food production in this small crowded island is negligible, and cannot possibly compare with that from the wide open spaces of Canada, Australia and New Zealand. In fact, the gross output of British farming, about £1,800 million per annum, is greater than that of Australia and New Zealand combined.[4] Very few British people would argue in favour of abolishing agriculture in either Australia or New Zealand, yet they all too readily assume that British agriculture is expendable.

But perhaps the underlying feeling is that Britain is predominantly an industrialized country, and that even if our agriculture has become mechanized and modernized, it cannot possibly make a contribution to the national economy comparable with that of the major industries. On this, too, the general opinion is not in line with the true facts. In 1961, the gross sales of the farming industry were roughly equal to those of the chemical industry, including exports.[5] The value of farm output was greater than that of either the coal industry or the motor industry.[6] Whatever problems agriculture may have – and there are many – it is already one of Britain's major industries, and it is still expanding.

Farming employs about a million farmers and farmworkers, which is 4% of Britain's labour force. The numbers directly employed in farming have been falling steadily, but the numbers indirectly employed in ancillary industries have been increasing. This is because agriculture, both here and in other European countries, is becoming 'capital intensive', i.e. making use of more

[4] NFU. 'Britain's Biggest Industry'. 1963.
[5] NEDC. 'Growth of U.K. Economy to 1966' Table 1.
[6] NFU. 'Britain's Biggest Industry'. 1963.

materials and services supplied by other industries – electric power, fuel oil, fertilizers, feeding stuffs, machinery, tools and equipment. In primitive agriculture, the farmer buys little and sells little. He builds his own house, makes his own tools and clothes, and produces very little food surplus to his own needs. But in 'capital intensive' agriculture, the farmer is a very large customer of other industries. It is estimated that British farmers spend £950 million per year on purchased materials and services. In addition, farmers and farmworkers spend another £850 million on their personal requirements.[7] Clearly, a prosperous agriculture provides a very valuable market for other industries.

The farming industry can also have a powerful stabilizing effect upon the economy. The problem of unemployment is still serious in certain areas, particularly in Scotland and Northern Ireland. There have been several periods of recession or slump, arising from the trade cycle which occurs in the United States and other capitalist countries, due to variations in the rate of private investment in industry. If, in a period of slump, one industry, or a group of industries, continues to operate at the same level as before, this helps to maintain purchasing power, which in turn keeps up the demand for goods from other industries. In Britain, the system of guaranteed farm prices has this effect. According to an international report by a group of economists : –

'National schemes of this kind for the stabilization of prices and incomes of agricultural and other primary producers provide a built-in stabilizer in the case of the highly industrialized countries. Thus, the fact that agricultural arrangements in the United States and the United Kingdom are now such as to prevent a collapse of farm incomes and farm purchasing power provides an important element in making these economies less prone to general fluctuations in their national incomes.'[8]

This preliminary survey shows that farming in the United Kingdom makes an important contribution to the national economy. It now produces two-thirds of our temperate food-

[7] NFU. 'Britain's Biggest Industry'. 1963.
[8] GATT. 'Trends in International Trade', par. 196.

stuffs, which are the basic constituents of our diet. It provides work on a large scale, both directly and indirectly, and helps to stabilize the level of employment. It can and should be classed as one of Britain's major industries.

CHAPTER 2

FARMING AND ECONOMIC GROWTH

OVER many years, the public has been aware that the British economy works erratically. There has been a balance of payments crisis every two or three years, and there have been several periods of severe unemployment, particularly in the winter of 1962-63. The various remedies applied by governments have become familiar – hire purchase restriction and de-restriction, credit squeeze and credit release, 'pay-pause' and 'guiding light'. To the discerning citizen, it has become obvious that the remedies which are good for the balance of payments are bad for unemployment, and vice-versa. But the underlying causes of economic sickness have remained obscure to the majority of ordinary people.

In 1962, the Government set up the National Economic Development Council, NEDC, with the task of studying these problems, and recommending ways of improving our economic performance. It was perhaps unfortunate that this body immediately became known by the undignified title of 'Neddy', because this was likely to detract from the fresh and constructive thinking revealed in their analysis. Unlike other economic surveys, the NEDC studied the economy as a living and developing organism, rather than as a static system. Specifically, they focussed attention on *economic* growth. They showed that this depends partly on the size of the labour force and the resources available, but principally upon the *productivity of labour*. The growth of productivity is determined by the level of capital investment and the application of new techniques. Whilst productivity in Britain has been rising by 1-2% per annum in the 1950's, in order industrial countries, including West Germany, France, Japan and Italy, it has been increasing by 4-5% per annum. As a result, Britain's share in world trade in manufactured goods has fallen from 21% in 1953 to 15% in 1962.[1] To reverse this trend, and to enable Britain to earn a living in the highly competitive conditions of today, the NEDC proposed a target of 4% growth per annum in the national output. This aim of faster economic growth provides a useful measure against which to evaluate the farming industry.

Referring to agriculture, the NEDC commented : –

'The industry contributes to growth in two ways. First, efficient production from the land helps the balance of payments by enabling us to displace imports of agricultural produce. Secondly, greater efficiency of resource utilization in agriculture contributes to growth.'[2]

Economic development does not proceed at a steady and even pace in all industries. There is, in fact, a wide range in the rate of growth, efficiency, productivity, technical achievement, and export effort of different industries. Based on the results of the previous five years, the NEDC selected seventeen industries which in that period contributed most to economic growth, and which were likely to contribute most in the period up to 1966. It is highly significant for farmers that agriculture was selected as one of the seventeen industries.

According to their rate of growth, the seventeen are grouped as follows : –

Fastest Growth – 'newer science-based industries' – chemicals, electricity, electronics and petroleum; and industries contributing most to exports – motor cars, heavy electrical machinery and machine tools.

Intermediate Growth – agriculture, building, constructional engineering, building materials, iron and steel, General Post Office and distribution.

Slower Growth – coal, gas, wool textiles, chocolate and sugar confectionery, paper and board.

The seventeen industries together cover about two-fifths of the

[1] NEDC. 'Conditions Favourable to Faster Growth', Par. 202.
[2] NEDC. 'Growth of U.K. Economy to 1966', Annex. 6.

national product. Between 1955-61 these industries had an average growth in output of 3.0%, compared with 2.5% for the rest of the economy. It is expected that in the period 1961-66 they will have an average rate of growth of 4.8%, well above the NEDC target. This means that if the rest of the economy could raise its rate of growth by 1% per annum, the economy as a whole would reach the 4% target.[3]

Agriculture contributes to economic growth both by increases in total output and by increases in productivity of labour. There are several ways in which this can be done. Suppose a dairy farmer has 60 cows being milked by 2 men, he could increase *output* by enlarging his herd to 90, and taking on 1 more man. Another alternative would be to increase *productivity*, by reorganizing his buildings and layout so that 1 man could manage the original 60 cows on his own. Yet another alternative would be to reorganize the unit in such a way that 2 men could look after 80 cows. This would represent an increase in both *output* and *productivity*. Developments of this kind are taking place every day in farming, and in this way the industry is contributing to the growth of the national economy.

Between 1956-61, the farming industry increased its output by 3.3% per annum. This compares with increases of 11.6% in petroleum, 8.6% in electricity, and 8.1% in motor vehicles. Other industries among the seventeen had a slower rate of growth than agriculture – crude steel 1.3% and gas 1.4%. For the period from 1961-66, the NEDC estimate that agriculture will continue to increase its output by 3.3% per annum. The largest increases, ranging from 7.5% to 13% are expected in chemicals, petroleum, electricity, machine tools, motor vehicles and heavy electrical machinery. So far as total output is concerned, the farming industry is making steady though not spectacular progress.[4]

But in *productivity of labour*, the farming industry is advancing very rapidly indeed. From 1956-61, productivity increased by over 5% per annum (output per man year), and between 1961-66 it is expected to increase by 6.1% per annum. These increases in productivity are comparable with those in chemicals, steel or motor vehicles – the industries which are making the

[3] NEDC. *Ibid*, Par. 114-118.
[4] NEDC. *Ibid*, Table 1.

greatest development. The reader will be prompted to ask if this means that the farm worker is producing as much wealth as the car worker or the chemical worker. This does not necessarily follow, because some industries have already reached a much more advanced level than others in technique and capital investment. In 1961, the chemical worker was producing about twice as much in value as the farm worker, but the worker in the motor industry was producing about the same.[5] The important point is that all three industries – chemicals, motor vehicles and farming – are developing their technique and organization, though at different levels.

The NEDC reports have been particularly valuable in drawing attention to the problems of economic growth. According to their analysis, agriculture is a valuable, growth-promoting industry, and, far from being curtailed, it is to be encouraged. But it does not follow from this that the NEDC has found the solution to all economic problems. Analysis is one thing: action is another. When it comes to an incomes policy, there is no agreement as to whose incomes are to be restrained, those of workers, employers, shareholders or professional people, and by what means. These and other thorny questions will harass politicians and trade union leaders for a long time to come.

So far, the productivity of farming has been considered from the outside, and from a statistical viewpoint. To those who work in farming, productivity and efficiency present a more confused picture. There is so much variation in systems and results between one farm and another, even in the same district. On similar land, one farmer grows 2 tons of corn to the acre, another only 1¼ tons. One dairy farmer obtains 1,000 gallons of milk per cow with a given level of concentrate feeding; another, with the same amount of feed, obtains only 600-700 gallons. Some farmers know their costs to the last ½d; others couldn't say whether they are making a profit or a loss. In every branch of farming, the leading producers are making twice as much margin as the average, whilst some of the stragglers are making a loss. If the average could be raised to the level of the best, the need for farm subsidies in their present form would soon disappear.

[5] NEDC. *Ibid*. Annex. 11, 12, 139 and 275.

These variations are caused partly by soil, climate, size and layout of farms, but even more by the skill, knowledge and managerial ability of the farmer. Like the rest of the community, farmers vary widely in their ability and determination, and this is reflected in their standard of farm management. Amongst the smaller farmers, there are many capable men who are prevented by lack of capital from applying the most advanced techniques. To raise farm productivity still further is a complex task, including the training of people, the investment of more capital, and the improvement in methods of production and marketing.

The uneven results in farming are characteristic of an industry that is in a state of transition. A report by the Food and Agriculture Organisation of the United Nations, FAO, on European Agriculture shows that Britain is not alone in experiencing these changes. The report concludes: –

'The evidence suggests that farmers in all European countries are travelling the same road, towards higher yields per unit of land, animals and labour, even if some are much further along the road than others, and various conditions may prevent the more backward from catching up with the more favoured regions and countries. . . .'

'We are still in the middle of a technological and managerial revolution. Its momentum is such that it will be carried forward in most countries of Europe at least in the period up to 1965.'[6]

The indications are that British farming is travelling along this road faster than most, and in this way it is contributing significantly to the growth of the national economy.

[6] FAO. 'European Agriculture in 1965', Part 1, par. 4.

CHAPTER 3

IMPORT SAVING

IN economic life, there is more and more pressure to 'keep up with the Jones' '. If West Germany, Japan, France and the United States were not forging ahead in industrial production, it would not be so urgent for Britain to increase the rate of economic growth. But the hard cold fact has to be faced that other nations are expanding rapidly, and the struggle for world markets is keener than ever before. The following table indicates the success of some of our principal competitors : –

Export of Manufactured Goods 1953-61[1]

Country	% Change in Price Index	% Change in Quantity
United Kingdom	+14%	+ 32%
West Germany	+ 5%	+191%
France	− 1%	+111%
Japan	− 9%	+290%
Italy	−21%	+345%

If these trends continued, Britain's share in world trade would dwindle further. For a country which was largely self-supporting, this might not matter unduly. But for Britain, depending heavily upon imports for food, raw materials and fuel, it could be disastrous. As conditions are at present, Britain cannot afford to opt out of the trade race.

Even before the war, imports of goods into the United Kingdom were considerably in excess of exports. But the gap was filled by what are called 'invisible items' – earnings from shipping and banking services, and large sums in interest and dividends on foreign investments accumulated in the era of colonial expansion. During the war, the Government commandeered many of these foreign assets, and sold them to pay for essential supplies. In recent years, the balance on 'invisible items' has shown only a

[1] NEDC. 'Conditions Favourable to Faster Growth', Table 8.

small credit, and in some years a debit. Faced with industrial expansion in competing countries, the Government has been compelled to stimulate exports and to restrain imports.

Foodstuffs have been one of the major groups of imports, amounting to about 30% of the total. Raw materials for industry are required in large quantities – cotton, wool, timber, rubber, iron ore, metals, chemicals. In the 1920-40 period, food and raw materials accounted for the greater part of our imports. But the pattern has been gradually changing. Today, a great volume of oil must be imported to sustain enormously increased motor traffic, and to operate heating systems in industries and homes. Even more striking is the steep rise in imports of manufactured goods. The figures show that these are now not far short of food imports, and by 1966 they are likely to exceed food imports :–

Imports 1961[2]
£ Millions

Food	1435
Drink and Tobacco	148
Materials	1131
Fuel	484
Manufactures	1200

There has been a world-wide trend for industrialized nations to trade amongst themselves in manufactured goods, to sell to each other cars, scooters, clothing, furniture and capital goods. Many of these imports have come into Britain over a high tariff wall. The duty on cars, for instance, is 25%. This represents a *pressure* upon the British market by competitors who are growing faster and producing more efficiently than Britain. In the case of Japanese and Italian exports, the industrialists have had a competitive advantage of lower wages. The British economy is therefore threatened both by an inadequate level of exports, and by an excessive flood of imports. Each time there is a period of trade expansion in Britain, imports tend to increase, because industry requires more imported materials, and because consumers have more income to spend and some of it is spent on imported goods. This leads to a worsening trade gap and a loss of gold reserves.

It is clear that in the face of these trading difficulties the farming industry is in a key position. The expansion of farming over

[2] NEDC. 'Growth of U.K. Economy to 1966'. Par. 281.

the last twenty-five years has greatly eased the balance of payments by reducing imports of food. This import saving has been between £300-400 million per annum,[3] a very substantial sum, equivalent to about 10% of the import bill, or about four-fifths of the value of oil imports. Without this increased food production, the trade gap would have been still more dangerous.

The expansion of farm production has, of course, been confined to temperate foodstuffs, suited to the British climate. The following figures show the proportion of these foods which are now home-produced:–

Temperate Foodstuffs – % Produced in United Kingdom[4]

Fresh Milk	100%
Poultry Meat	98%
Eggs	97%
Pork	96%
Barley	84%
Temperate Vegetables	83%
Beef and Veal	76%
Temperate Fruits	65%
Cheese	46%
Mutton and Lamb	43%
Wheat	37%
Bacon	36%
Butter	11%

Britain is well on the way to being self-sufficient in eight out of the twelve products. But we rely heavily upon imports for wheat, bacon, butter and lamb.

Wheat production in Britain has greatly increased, but due to our wet summers, it is difficult to produce sufficient of the hard wheats which are preferred for bread-making. Canada, with the advantage of consistently hot dry summers, has specialized in the production of hard wheat on the prairies. Their Wheat Marketing Board exercises very careful control over seed, and imposes strict standards of grading for the grain, with the result that they have secured an unrivalled reputation for high-grade wheat.

Denmark is our chief supplier of bacon, as well as sending some butter. It is a country of small farms, on which a very

[3] NFU. 'Britain's Biggest Industry'. 1963.
[4] NFU. *Ibid.*

high output per acre has been achieved by the application of skill and technical knowledge, and by a network of co-operative organizations. They have specialized in breeding Landrace pigs for the Wiltshire Cure, and they turn out bacon of a uniformly high standard, which is very popular with British shopkeepers and housewives.

New Zealand, endowed with an adequate rainfall and a sunny climate, in which the grass grows for ten months of the year, has specialized in dairy farming and sheep rearing. Their farmers excel in these forms of pastoral farming, and high standards of grading are maintained by national marketing organizations, which export butter, lamb and wool to Britain and elsewhere.

Two other nations have been very large suppliers of agricultural produce to Britain – Australia and the Argentine. As the world's largest wool producer, Australia is first and foremost a sheep and cattle country, but in certain areas wheat is grown on a large scale, and some localities are very well suited to fruit production, for drying and canning.

The Argentine, famous for chilled beef, has built up a very valuable export trade, based on the fertile plain, known as the Pampas, which stretches in a semi-circle for about 300 miles around Buenos Aires. Here, great herds of cattle, based largely on Angus and Shorthorn stock from Britain, can be kept on pasture all the year round. A system of abattoir-freezing plants, the 'Frigoricos', at the ports, makes possible an efficient export trade to Britain, Germany and other countries. The Argentine is also the world's largest exporter of hides.

These exporting countries – Canada, Denmark, New Zealand, Australia and the Argentine – are advanced nations, in which modern farming methods are used, and in which the farmers have a high standard of knowledge and skill. Their efforts are re-inforced by efficient marketing organizations, either sponsored or supervised by the state, which ensure that the products are well graded and presented. These countries have earned a world-wide reputation for their farm production.

But it would be an error to assume that by contrast British farm production is negligible. As mentioned earlier, the value of farm production in Britain is greater than that of Australia and New Zealand combined. So far as grain production is concerned,

British output is surprisingly large compared with that of our two largest suppliers : —

Grain Production — 1000 Metric Tons[5]

Country	Average 1961-63	Types of Grain
United Kingdom	11,042	Wheat, Barley, Oats, Rye
Canada	24,022	Wheat, Barley, Oats, Rye and Maize
Australia	10,429	Wheat, Barley Oats, Rye Maize, Mixed Corn, Rice

The grain output of our small island is 40-45% that of Canada, and approximately the same as that of Australia.

In meat production, too, British output compares favourably with that of Australia, New Zealand and the Argentine.

Meat Production — 1000 Metric Tons[6]

Country	Average 1961-63	
United Kingdom	1,825	Beef, Veal, Pork, Mutton, Lamb
Australia	1,500	Beef, Veal, Pork, Mutton, Lamb
New Zealand	755	Beef, Veal, Pork, Mutton, Lamb
Argentine	2,477	Beef, Veal, Pork, Mutton, Lamb

British output is greater than that of either Australia or New Zealand, and is equivalent to about three-quarters of the Argentine total. These few facts confirm that so far as temperate foodstuffs are concerned, Britain is now a large-scale producer.

The supply of tropical products is drawn from a wide circle of countries — tea from India, Ceylon and Pakistan; sugar from Australia, the West Indies, Mauritius and Fiji; oil seeds for making margarine from Nigeria and other African countries. Cocoa comes from Ghana and Nigeria, and coffee from Brazil and some African countries. Citrus fruits are imported from Spain, Israel and South Africa. The majority of suppliers are members of the Commonwealth, and in many cases their trade with Britain is of decisive importance to their economies. Exports of tea, for example, from Ceylon, India and Pakistan amounted to £180 million in 1960, of which £100

[5] FAO. *Production Year Book* 1963. Tables 12-20 (1 Metric Ton Equals 2,205 lbs).

[6] FAO. *Production Year Book* 1963. Table 80B.

million was purchased by the United Kingdom.[7] These less developed countries rely upon earnings from tea and other exports to pay for desperately needed capital goods to facilitate their economic development.

From these facts, it is clear that Britain's imported food supplies are big business, both for the importing firms, who handle the trade, and for the supplying countries. For the suppliers of temperate foodstuffs, Denmark, New Zealand, and Canada, this trade is essential for maintaining the relatively high standard of living they enjoy. For the suppliers of tropical products, it is an indispensable lifeline by which they hope to lift themselves out of poverty.

It has been demonstrated that the expansion of British farming has brought about a substantial import saving. But the critical reader will realize that this has not been done without cost. The Government has been paying between £200-300 million per year in farm subsidies and grants. It is reasonable to ask whether this has been an expensive way of saving imports, and whether these resources could have been better spent otherwise. A serious study of this subject was published in 1958 by Professor E. A. G. Robinson.[8]

He estimates that agricultural import saving was worth about £300 million per annum during the 1950's. There have also been import duties, averaging 25%, on about £200 million worth of industrial imports. This has enabled home industries to retain a larger share of the home market, and has resulted in import saving of about £200 million. The combined import saving on agricultural and industrial products, brought about by farm subsidies and tariffs, is reckoned at about £500 million.

Professor Robinson calculates that if protection were removed from both industry and agriculture, it is probable that imports would increase by £500 million per year. This poses the question: could Britain increase her exports sufficiently to pay for this very large increase in imports? It would require an increase in foreign earnings of 15%. But this would need an increase in the *volume* of exports of very much more than 15% – for two reasons. Firstly, the price of British exports would have to be

[7] The Council of Europe. 'The Commonwealth and Europe in 1962'. Table VI. p.31.
[8] The Three Banks Review. Dec. 1958.

lowered very considerably, by 20-25% to capture additional markets, and to compensate for this a larger quantity would have to be exported. Secondly, the majority of manufactured goods use some imported materials (the average import-content is about 15%) and to allow for this a still larger quantity of exports would be needed. Professor Robinson concludes that to reach the required target of 15% more foreign earnings, the *volume* of exports would have to be raised by 50%. It is very doubtful if Britain has the physical or organizational resources to undertake a task of this magnitude.

Even if it was physically possible, there are other serious difficulties. In Professor Robinson's words: '90% of the world's export trade in manufactures is in the hands of the "big eleven", and an attempt to increase our share by 50% would imply on average a 12½% reduction in their exports – if world trade remained the same. Although foreign importers would gain from our cheaper manufactured goods, their exporters would lose, and most states would respond in one way or another.' It is almost certain that the competing nations would retaliate, by imposing tariffs, quotas and import levies, or by devaluing their currency, which would cancel out the advantage of lower British prices.

It is most unlikely that British manufacturers could attain the 20-25% reduction in export prices without a devaluation of the pound. The effect of this would be to make British exports cheaper for foreigners to buy, and in this way to stimulate the export trade. But it also makes imports correspondingly more expensive, and if imported food became 20-25% dearer, British agriculture would be able to compete on equal terms with all comers.

Professor Robinson reaches the conclusion 'That we are on the whole using our resources economically, but achieving that result by somewhat unorthodox and roundabout methods'. So it appears that during the 1950's, the farm subsidies resulted in an import saving of about £300 million per year, and stimulated the production of food which would have been extremely difficult, if not impossible, to pay for if it had been imported.

The outlook for foreign trade in the next five or ten years still seems to be precarious, as indicated by the sterling crisis at the end of 1964. Britain is the largest purchaser of food supplies on the world market. In the past, this gave us a powerful bargaining position, in securing food supplies cheaply and in placing our exports abroad. Today, our competitors can frequently offer to the food exporting countries manufactured goods which are cheaper, better or with more favourable credit and service facilities than ours. In addition, a number of rapidly developing countries, including Japan, the Soviet Union and China, are beginning to buy food from our traditional sources, so that pressure on these supplies is increasing. In these new circumstances, excessive dependence on imported food is no longer a trading advantage: it can be a very serious danger. Some industrialists have drawn the conclusion that home production of food should be expanded. At the Oxford Farming Conference in January 1965, Mr Paul Chambers, Chairman of ICI said that food imports worth £250 million a year were currently vulnerable, and represented a fair target for a competitive British agriculture. Every part of this home market captured by farmers from foreign competitors would make an immediate contribution to the balance of payments.[9] The National Farmers Union have estimated that increased farm production since 1938 is now equivalent to a saving of £400 million per year on the balance of payments.[10] If farm production increased still further, this saving might be raised to £600-700 million in the next few years. Against this background, restriction of farm production would seem to be an extremely short-sighted policy.

Increased farm production would require some increase in imported materials, which are used in farming as they are in industrial production. Farmers use petrol and diesel fuel, which are imported, though much of it is refined in Britain. Some phosphate fertilizers are imported and practically all our potash fertilizers. Imports of maize for animal feeding are the largest single item, amounting to about $2\frac{1}{4}$ million tons per year, plus 2-3 million tons of other animal feeding stuffs.

Against these imported materials should be set the export of farm produce from Britain to other countries. This includes barley for malting, high grade seeds, pedigree livestock, wool, and, when markets are favourable, some meat and eggs. These exports have gradually increased to a total of about £60 million[11]

[9] *Farmers Weekly*, Jan. 8, 1965.
[10] NFU. British Agriculture Looks Ahead, p.7.
[11] NFU. *Ibid*, p.8.

per year, and could increase further. In Europe, there is a shortage of meat, especially beef, which is more in demand as standards of living rise. If supplies in the United Kingdom were sufficient, an export trade could be built up. Many nations are working to improve their farm livestock, for example, France, Yugoslavia, and Italy, and are buying British cattle, sheep, pigs and poultry, particularly where performance records are available. New technical processes for drying and preserving milk and eggs, with perfect retention of freshness and flavour, could make possible the export of these protective foods, particularly to undeveloped countries. Home farming also provides a testing ground and shop window for the agricultural machinery industry, which has been highly successful in the export trade, with sales amounting to £165 million per year, making Britain the world's second largest exporter.[12] With agricultural development going on in many parts of the world, there is a growing opportunity for agricultural exports from countries, like Britain, which have an advanced and mechanized farming industry. This is a further contribution, in addition to saving imports, which British agriculture could and should make to the balance of payments problem.

[12] NFU. *Ibid*, p.8.

CHAPTER 4

FOOD AND HEALTH

ECONOMIC growth and industrial efficiency obviously depend upon a fit and energetic labour force. A plentiful supply of food at reasonable prices is essential. If food supplies are inadequate, health and vigour are gradually undermined, and industrial production begins to suffer.

In Britain, food is the largest item in most family budgets, accounting for 35% of expenditure on the average.[1] The ordinary housewife demands a wide choice of high quality food when she goes shopping, and she hopes to find it at reasonable prices. It is no exaggeration to say that the price of food determines whether or not her weekly budget will balance.

The price of food is also closely watched by the Government. Food is the heaviest weight in the cost of living index, which directly and indirectly influences the wages of millions of workers. In the last twenty-five years, food subsidies have been a valuable means of keeping down the cost of living. Imported food from some of the world's most efficient producers, particularly those in the Commonwealth, has been allowed in free of tariffs or duties. At the same time, the system of guaranteed prices has enabled farmers in the United Kingdom to accept lower prices than they could have done on a free market. Where market prices are below the guarantee, the Government has made up the difference. In the financial sense, farm subsidies have resulted in a transfer of wealth from the taxpayer to the food consumer. Since rich and poor alike consume food, but those with small incomes and large families are exempt from taxation, this represents a redistribution of wealth in favour of the less well-off sections of the population. The Agriculture Act of 1947 was, in fact, much more than the means to farming prosperity; it

[1] Cost of Living Index. Report of Advisory Committee. Cmd. 1657. 1962.

was also the means to a food and nutrition policy to benefit the whole nation.

Some indication of the effectiveness of the Act can be seen by comparing food prices in Britain with those of other European countries. The following table shows the differences in price for a number of staple foods.

Retail Prices – October 1962[2]

	Milk Pint	White Wheat Bread lb	Beef Sirloin lb	Pork Shoulder lb	Butter lb	Eggs doz	Pota- toes lb
United Kingdom	8½d	7½d	5/6½	3/10½	3/5	2/6 - 4/5	3½d
Denmark	6½d	1/1	4/11	4/8½	4/1	4/2½	3½d
France	6½d	7d	8/0½	–	6/2½	4/4½	3½d
W. Germany	–	1/0	6/2	3/6	5/10½	4/6	2½d
Italy	6½d	10½d	7/11½	8/9	6/9½	5/11	5d

The table shows that Britain and Denmark had markedly lower food prices, particularly for beef, pork and butter, and the British price for bread was much lower than that of all the other countries except France. For milk, the British price is higher, but it should be noted that our standards of milk hygiene are the highest in Europe, and ours is the only country to have a complete daily delivery system. Clearly, these relatively low food prices have been of incalculable benefit to the health of the people.

Low food prices are also a great advantage to British industrialists. They can pay a lower level of wages than would be required if food prices were high, and this helps to keep down manufacturing costs compared with those of foreign firms. When the Common Market negotiations were in progress, one of the central points in dispute was the British system of agricultural support. The European countries objected to this, partly because they insisted that there must be a uniform agricultural policy for all members, but principally because farm support gave British industry a competitive advantage. If we had joined the Common Market, farm support would have been abolished, and the price of food in the shops would have risen by at least 10%. Further,

[2] *International Labour Review*. Supplement July 1963.

under the rules of the European Community, Britain would have had to impose levies on food imports from the Commonwealth, and other outside countries, to bring their prices into line with those ruling inside the Community, and the levies would have been passed over to a European fund to help backward agricultural areas. With our very large imports of food, this would have placed a crippling burden on Britain, and raised the price of food still further.

So far, food has been considered in rather impersonal terms, as a kind of fuel to keep industrial workers running efficiently. But nutrition has much wider implications than this. Food is the first elementary need of humanity, and in any community, should the food supply break down, disaster would occur within a very short time. Good food is one of the foundations upon which the health of the people can be built up – strong and energetic children, workers with stamina and concentration, old people fortified for as long as possible against decline. Without good nutrition, the other activities of the community are correspondingly weakened, education and learning, sport and entertainment, industry and commerce. So it would seem reasonable that in a civilized country a sufficient, well-balanced diet should be available to every citizen without exception, just as a plentiful supply of pure water is taken for granted as necessary for the good of one and all.

It is ironical to recall that in pre-war days, in spite of the so-called 'cheap food' policy, the nutrition and health of the people were very unsatisfactory. In 1938, Sir John Boyd Orr proved conclusively that 50% of the population, including a high proportion of the nation's children, were in varying degrees undernourished.[3] Special surveys of schoolchildren in London and Durham showed that four-fifths had signs of rickets, the serious bone disease directly related to poverty and malnutrition.[4] It is impossible to estimate the indirect effects of poor diet, in lowering resistance to disease, in retarding the mental and physical development of children at school, and in robbing men and women of energy and confidence. Those who suffered unemployments in the 1930's can never forget the era of the 'Hunger Marches'.

[3] Sir John Boyd Orr. 'Food, Health & Income'.
[4] G. D. H. Cole. *The Condition of Britain*. p.109. (Gollancz.)

It took a war and the threat of blockade and defeat to bring about a change in the official attitude to nutrition. To sustain the war effort, soldiers and workers had to be fit, and their wives and children had to be properly cared for. The Government took control of all food supplies, and instituted rationing. Workers in heavy industries, mothers and babies were given priority. By the end of the war, the population as a whole was better nourished than they had ever been in peacetime. Though dull and monotonous, war-time diet provided the essentials to all families, whereas previously several millions had been subsisting on bread, margarine and tea.

It was in this period that Sir William Beveridge drafted his famous report on the social services, which provided the blueprint for the welfare state. His conception of 'freedom from want' was to apply to every section of the community, as a protection against the hazards of an industrial society, such as unemployment, sickness, accident, or old age. It is obvious that freedom from want must include freedom from hunger and malnutrition. In positive terms, this means that a diet adequate for health should be guaranteed to every citizen.

In the last two decades, great progress has been made towards this aim, through higher wages, children's allowances, school milk and meals. The widespread teaching of domestic science has encouraged better cooking and planning of meals. The results, in the height, weight and fitness of our children, are dramatic. These higher standards of nutrition are accepted as normal and necessary, but even today they are not applied consistently and universally. In the winter of 1963, 900,000 people were out of work, and on the present rates of unemployment benefit, it is likely that several million children were affected by malnutrition, to a greater or less extent. This also seems to be accepted as 'normal'.

It is certain that a proportion of elderly people, living on the old age pension, are seriously undernourished, particularly when a bitterly cold winter forces them to spend much more on heating. There have been disquieting reports that diet in some hospitals is unbalanced and badly prepared. The Platt Report found that standards of hygiene in food handling were defective, and that in many hospitals nearly half the food prepared for patients was thrown away as swill.[5] The tradition that prison diet should be unpleasant results in a lack of vitamins and other essential elements, so that the physical fitness of prisoners is impaired. The conclusion cannot be escaped that in our society freedom from malnutrition is denied to the weakest members – the very young, the very old, the sick and the delinquent.

This impression is confirmed by the figures published by the Ministry of Agriculture on food consumption and expenditure. Surprisingly, our diet has not altered a great deal in terms of energy value over the last twenty-five years. The average intake of calories per head per day has risen from 3,000 pre-war to 3,150 in 1960, an increase of only 3%. The quality of our diet, however, has improved greatly. The proportion of protein has risen by 17%, calcium by 60%, vitamin A by 26%, vitamin C by 5% and iron by 22%. The average figures, as might be expected, conceal wide differences between income groups. The survey divides the population according to the gross weekly income of the head of the household. The expenditure per week is shown to vary from 37s 8d for class 'A', earning £30 a week or more, to 27s 10d for old age pensioners. But the most startling differences are between families with no children and families with four or more children. Between 1956-60, a childless couple in class 'A' spent 45s per head per week, whereas a family with four children in classes 'C' or 'D' spent only 17s 1d per head.[6] The survey also shows that the diet of children in these large families was deficient in protein and calcium, two of the most vital elements for young and growing children. The figures confirm that while, on the average, the quality of diet has improved, there are still submerged groups in the population, particularly amongst children, who are not receiving an adequate diet on account of poverty.

For those with sufficient money to pay for food, there has been an improvement in the range and quality of food on sale. Housewives have gradually been making their preferences felt, and these have been reflected in both production and distribution. The term 'quality' covers a wide range of factors which are now being demanded by consumers. The more discriminating buyers

[5] *The Guardian*. Feb. 22, 1964.
[6] Ministry of Agriculture. Food Consumption & Expenditure 1962.

are interested in high standards of grading, which can be relied upon week after week, for instance, in Danish bacon or New Zealand lamb. There is a strong preference for leanness and tenderness in meat, and this has increased the demand for broiler chickens, light-weight pork, and young beef. Housewives are eager to secure freshness, particularly in eggs, and will pay a high premium for unstamped eggs which they hope have come straight from the farm. The fresh flavour of quick-frozen fish and vegetables is a big selling point. Fresh cream is also building up a large trade, especially at weekends. The public, with more money in their pockets than in the past, no longer want to buy bruised or blemished fruit at a cheap price; they prefer to pay more for attractive and well-graded fruit. There is a strong demand for well-flavoured English fruits, such as strawberries, raspberries, blackcurrants and Cox's apples, when these are available. There is a taste for more variety in food, including mushrooms, many types of home-made and imported cheese, imported wines etc. Many housewives have realized the health-giving qualities of milk, salads, tomatoes, oranges and lemons, and consumption of these products has been rising. The rush of modern life causes many women to make use of pre-packs, frozen and tinned foods, cooked meats and pies, and the supermarkets cater particularly for the demand for these convenience foods. This brief list indicates the high standards demanded from the food producer, both at home and abroad.

This means that the task of the farmer is more exacting than in the past. He is required to produce and market his goods to an accurate specification as to size, type, freshness, flavour and finish. Ht must also pack and present his goods attractively, or alternatively send them to an organization which can efficiently take on this job for him. He must plan production so that he has consignments ready at regular intervals to meet the needs of the distributor.

For many years, the food exporting countries have carefully studied the consumers' requirements, and have provided well-graded and standardized products. British farmers were very slow to adopt modern selling methods, but more recently they have begun to catch up. Many organizations are now trying to put high-grade British products on the market, and to win the acceptance of the public. The Milk Marketing Board, with their famous 'Drinka Pinta' advertisements and Dairy Festivals have been foremost in this drive. Many local associations are trying to produce and market quality bacon, quality pork, farm-fresh eggs etc. The British producer has an immense advantage in having the market on his doorstep, particularly for providing fresh milk, cream, eggs, meat, fruit and vegetables. The British climate, with its alternating sun and rain, enables us to grow fine-flavoured fruit and vegetables, which mature and ripen slowly. But good produce has in the past been spoiled by bad grading and presentation, and lack of uniformity. If these defects could be overcome, the growing demand for quality foods of all kinds presents an unlimited opportunity for British farmers.

An urban society requires an extremely complex system of food distribution. Transport, marketing, processing, refrigeration, grading, packaging, retailing – these operations require very efficient planning, and large capital outlay, particularly for perishable products. The tendency has been for big organizations to take over more and more of the food trade, with chains of shops or supermarkets. Some of these firms are also handling imports, and entering directly into production. On present trends, it is likely that food distribution will gradually come under the control of fewer and larger concerns. This can be dangerous both for farmers and consumers. It could mean that farmers are unable to bargain for a fair share of the final price of the product. It is doubtful if farmers' groups, organized locally, would be strong enough to obtain fair terms, unless there were Marketing Boards with power to act as the first buyer. For the consumer, the danger of 'supermarketization' is that the choice of food may be limited to what is convenient to package and advertise, rather than providing a wide choice of varied foods. There may also be excessive pressure to sell ready-to-eat packaged foods, rather than the most fresh and nutritious products. There is, in addition, the possibility that prices may be fixed by unwritten agreement between a few large chains, rather than at the lowest possible price consistent with an efficient service. Where a product is supplied by a few very large firms, price competition is usually limited. The housewife is attracted to the supermarket by pleasant surroundings, convenience and attractively packaged products, but it may not be easy for her to judge whether she is paying too highly for these services, and taking home food of mediocre quality. If the supply of food is regarded as a social necessity, rather than a commercial enterprise, it seems essential that the interests of both producer and consumer should be protected. For this purpose, National Commodity Commissions, may be needed, with wider powers than the traditional Marketing Boards, including the power to regulate farm and retail prices, where necessary, to promote high standards of quality, and to enforce measures of hygiene in the preparation and sale of food.

The evidence suggests that the demand for high quality food of all kinds is going to increase, as the standard of living rises. In addition, the total quantity of food required is bound to rise, partly as a result of higher incomes and partly as a result of rising population. If through social policy old age pensions and children's allowances were raised, the food consumption of these groups would also increase. The NEDC forecast that food consumption will go on rising by 2% per annum in the period up to 1970.[7] Looking further ahead, to 2000, the Registrar General estimates that the population of England and Wales will increase by 18 millions or 37%. To provide this enlarged population with a first-rate diet, a very substantial increase in food supplies will be needed.

[7] NEDC. Joint Advisory Committee on Agriculture.

CHAPTER 5

THE REAL COST OF SUBSIDIES

OVER the last twenty years, agriculture has received a substantial sum in Government support, amounting to between £200-300 million per year, during the 1950's, and reaching a peak of £340 million in 1961/62.[1] These subsidies have aroused hostility and criticism amongst the general public, who feel that they are being compelled to dip into their pockets to provide a comfortable standing of living for feather-bed farmers. Many economists have poured scorn on the industry for accepting this assistance, with the implication that farmers are living 'on the dole'. It is this issue which, more than any other, deprives farmers of recognition and respect by the rest of the community.

But farm support is not a mere 'hand-out' to farmers. It has, in fact, a threefold effect on the national economy, firstly keeping down the cost of food to the consumer, secondly reducing the volume of imports, and thirdly promoting increased productivity within the farming industry itself. These three results have benefited the whole community quite as much as they have benefited farmers. When the 1947 Agriculture Act was passed food was very scarce and foreign trade was disrupted by the war. The aim of the Government was to ensure adequate food supplies, both home produced and imported: to get the best of both worlds by an open-door policy for farm products from overseas, combined with guaranteed prices to encourage expansion of farming inside Britain. The main objectives have been successfully achieved. The cost of food has remained relatively low, compared with other European countries, and nutritional standards have improved. Increased farm output in Britain has made possible a major saving on imports, and lessened the strain on the

[1] NFU. Information Service. *Annual Reviews.*

balance of payments. At the same time, the steady improvement in farm land, equipment and buildings has been a long-term investment, enabling agriculture to contribute to the growth of the national economy. All these consequences have followed from the system of farm support.

Yet, paradoxically, in spite of government aid, many farmers have been suffering financial stringency. Particularly in the last six to seven years, their incomes have not kept pace with those of the rest of the community. Only a minority of farmers, about 6% of the total, earn more than £3,000 per year.[2] Their expensive cars, which stand out at agricultural shows and other public gatherings, attract the critical attention of the townsman, who draws the conclusion that all farmers are profiteering out of the subsidies. But, in reality, about 60% of farmers are earning less than £1,000 a year, which is not high in relation to the effort put into the work, the hazards of nature, and the large amount of capital invested. Moreover, two-thirds of this group, or 40% of all farmers, earn less than £600 a year,[3] an income insufficient to provide a reasonable standard of living for these men and their families, and certainly insufficient to provide a margin for essential capital improvements. These facts suggest that all is not well in the working of the subsidy system. To those who look below the surface, it is clear that there is some misdirection of government aid as between those who need it and those who do not; there is also some wastage and some leakage of subsidies to interests outside farming. It is necessary to examine these problems in order to arrive at a complete evaluation of the system of farm support.

This system was laid down by the Agriculture Act of 1947, the most ambitious farm legislation ever undertaken in this country. The Act was passed by the Labour Government, 'for the purpose of promoting and maintaining, by the provision of guaranteed prices and assured markets . . . a stable and efficient agricultural industry'. The short-term aim of the Act was increased production, to ease the lot of the tightly rationed housewife. The long-term aim was greater stability of farm-prices than in the past, and fairer returns for farmers, farmworkers and landlords.

[2] NFU. Farm Accounts Scheme.
[3] NFU. *Ibid.*

Farm support under the Act is of two distinct kinds – production grants and price guarantees. The production grants are a contribution towards capital improvements, including fertilizers and lime, ploughing up of old grassland, water supplies, drainage and ditching. A group of grants are designed to help hill farmers. The Farm Improvement Scheme of 1957 provided grants of one third of the cost of composite improvements to fixed equipment and buildings, and in 1958 the Small Farmer Scheme enabled farms between 20-100 acres to obtain grants for capital improvements and working capital, to a total of £1,000, providing they followed a farm plan worked out with the National Agricultural Advisory Service. These production grants rose gradually during the 1950's from about £50 million per year to about £107 million, and they now represent 30-40% of agricultural support.[4]

The production grants have been a strong incentive to make good the vast backlog of neglect and dilapidation which accumulated in the years of farming depression. The National Farm Survey, conducted by the Government under the stress of war in 1941-43, showed that in England and Wales 47% of farmhouses and 63% of farm buildings had no mains water supply, and 73% of farm holdings had no electricity supply. Only about 40% of farm roads, fences, ditches and field drainage systems were in good condition. The use of manures and fertilizers was inadequate on 40% of the arable land and on more than half the pasture land.[5] Over the last twenty years, the production grants, plus the personal investment of farmers and landlords, have raised enormously the fertility of the land, the comfort of farmhouses and cottages, and the efficiency of buildings, yards and layouts. This represents a significant and permanent increase in the nation's productive resources, similar to the investment in new coal mines and nuclear power stations, or to the modernization of shipyards. The principle of Government aid to industry for such purposes, in both nationalized and privately-owned industries, is well established, and the application of this principle to farming is usually accepted by the public, once it is explained to them.

But the greater part of Government aid to farming has been in the form of guaranteed prices, and it is this form of support

[4] Annual Review 1965. Cmd. 2621.
[5] Ministry of Agriculture. *National Farm Survey* 1942.

which can rightly be called a subsidy to the industry, and which is most often the subject of controversy. The price guarantees apply to wheat, barley, oats, sugar beet, potatoes, eggs, cattle, sheep, pigs, milk and wool. Both milk and sugar beet are purchased direct from farmers by Marketing Boards at fixed prices. For other products, there are deficiency payment schemes, whereby free marketing is combined with Government assistance to bring the farmer's return up to the minimum, or 'standard price'. For example, in the case of pigs, sheep and cattle, farmers sell through markets or direct to factories and processing firms, obtaining the best price they can. All such sales are certified, and the farmers receive the difference between their price and the standard price, if market prices are low, or may have a deduction made if their prices are above the standard price. Adjustments in the deficiency payments are made as the prices of feeding stuffs rise and fall. In the case of pigs, a standard quantity is applied, whereby if the number of pigs certified for slaughter rises above a certain point, the rate of guarantee is automatically reduced. The intention underlying all these schemes is that the farmer should be encouraged to sell his products to the best advantage on a competitive market, whilst being assured of a minimum or 'floor price'. The Agriculture Act of 1957 reinforced the system by giving longer-term guarantees. The Government undertook not to reduce the total value of the guarantees by more than $2\frac{1}{2}\%$ per year, allowing for cost changes.

During the 1950's, the total sum of farm support was gradually falling, and as farm output was rising, the proportion of subsidy was declining. But in 1961/62, Parliament was alarmed by a sudden and unpredicted rise of £60 million in the subsidy bill for meat. This focussed attention on one of the defects of the scheme, that fluctuations in imports could cause the subsidy bill to get out of hand. The pressure of imports is a major influence in the sale of meat and grain. In 1961, rather large shipments of Argentine beef coincided with slightly increased home supplies, the market price slumped, and the bill for deficiency payments was sharply increased. In the case of grain, timing is particularly important. If large shiploads of American maize arrive at the time of the British harvest, they can have a strongly depressive effect on the barley market, since maize and barley have a competing use for animal feeding. If barley prices are pushed down, the subsidy is increased and the Government has to foot the bill. This 'open end' to the subsidy system is now recognized as harmful both to British and foreign producers. In June 1963, the Minister of Agriculture, Mr Soames, said : –

'We must make arrangements to control the level of imports, in consultation with our overseas suppliers. We have a firm obligation to many of them, but believe that arrangements to safeguard this market from undue pressures, to avoid disruption, are as much in their interest as to home producers.'[6]

This heralded a new policy of co-ordinating imports with home production, by agreements with supplying countries on the quantity and timing of imports. A Bacon Agreement has been concluded with Denmark and other suppliers, whereby the British market is shared in agreed proportions. Unfortunately, the British share is only 36%, due to weaknesses in the bacon industry here. Consultations have been held with the Argentine and other meat suppliers, to even out their shipments. The Government has prepared a system of levies to regulate the price of grain imports. The effect of these measures can be to protect the British market against dumping, and close up this 'open end' to the subsidy bill.

But there is another 'open end' which can inflate the subsidy bill even more than erratic imports, namely, disorganized systems of marketing, as a result of which wholesalers or retailers can divert the subsidy to increase their profit margins. It is significant that for those products which have Marketing Boards the subsidies have been falling : –

Product	1959/60	1963/64[7]
	£ Millions	£ Millions
Eggs	33.1	20.2
Potatoes	1.0	0.4
Milk	8.5	Nil

Practically the whole of the increase in subsidies has been concentrated upon fatstock and cereals, which have no centralized

[6] *Farmers Weekly*, June 28, 1963.
[7] *Annual Review* 1965. Cmd. 2621.

Marketing Boards:--

Product	1959/60 £ Millions	1963/64[8] £ Millions
Cereals	58.4	77.1
Fatstock	50.9	80.6

This increase in subsidies has been due, in part, to variations in imports, but even more to chaotic marketing. In the case of meat, the wholesale markets are unstable, and prices tend to fluctuate out of all proportion to changes in supply. In theory, when supply increases, prices in the shops should fall, customers should buy more, and supply and demand come into equilibrium. But, in practice, this does not happen. Housewives do not know that supplies are higher and that wholesale prices are lower, and they tend to buy the same amount of meat every week. Many butchers, accordingly, do not lower their prices, and, as the wholesale price has fallen, their profit margin widens. Lack of refrigeration facilities in many of the big markets magnifies the fluctuations, because any meat that comes in must be sold quickly, even at give-away prices. Thus, the effect of a slump in meat prices is that butchers' profit margins increase, and the Government has a heavy bill for deficiency payments, which are going indirectly to the meat traders, instead of giving the housewife the benefit of lower prices in the shops.

The Verdon Smith Committee, set up by the Government to study meat marketing, did not consider that any radical changes were required. But many farmers are convinced that there should be a Meat Marketing Board, or Commodity Commission, with power to provide refrigerating and storage facilities, and with power to buy meat and withdraw it from the market in times of excessive supply, and release it when supplies were scarce. This would make it possible to plug up this 'open end' to the subsidy bill, and prevent Government support being diverted to other interests.

Apart from the question of 'open ends', the guaranteed price system has not provided farmers with a satisfactory return, particularly in the last ten years. Productivity per man has been rising by 5-6%, yet farmers' real incomes have remained almost

[8] *Ibid.*

static if allowance is made for the fall in the value of the £. Prices of the principal farm products have remained stationary, or even been reduced, whilst costs have been rising steadily. By working harder and producing a larger output, farmers as a whole have managed to stay in the same place. Those with plenty of capital and a large acreage of crops have fared better than those depending mainly on livestock production. In an inflationary situation, with costs and prices of everything else moving upwards, farmers have been the odd man out, with their prices held down. Their position has been made worse by the standard quantity arrangements applied to pigs and cereals, whereby if they raise production above a certain level, their price is automatically cut. As individual farmers try to lower their cost by producing more, the group as a whole is penalised. The 1957 Agriculture Act, which was intended to give farmers long-term security, has in practice been used to apply a very harsh income squeeze. Up to a point, this pressure has stimulated farmers to seek more efficient methods of production, but if carried too far, it can exhaust and weaken the industry, besides creating great bitterness and unrest.

Meanwhile, the cost to the Exchequer of farm support has been falling. The production grants have remained steady at about £107 million for the last five years. These grants are an extremely valuable long-term investment in modernizing the industry, an investment which will pay off in terms of rising food supplies. In the same period, the price subsidies have declined from a peak of £225 million in 1961/62 to £150 million (forecast) for 1963/64, a drop of nearly one third, whilst farm output has been steadily rising.[9] The conclusion is inescapable that the farming community have not been receiving a fair reward for their efforts. It is their low incomes which are providing the public with cheap food.

There is a further problem in the wide inequality between farmers themselves. between the 5-6% earning over £3,000 per year, and the 60% earning less than £1,000 a year to cover return on capital and the labour of the farmer and his wife. This inequality is likely to increase further with the growth of farming companies, operating very large units, either in arable farm-

[9] *Ibid.*

ing, or with intensive livestock, and with the tendency towards vertical integration of farming and processing activities. The large units, with access to unlimited capital from the banks and the City of London, will be able to apply the latest techniques, employ high-grade labour, and obtain the economies of large-scale buying and selling. In the production of eggs, it is possible that one producer will soon secure control of 20% of the market. Under the existing system, this producer would receive several million £s a year in subsidy. It is inconceivable that Parliament, or the general public, could accept this situation for long. This dilemma, which is already acute in the poultry industry, may spread to other branches within a few years, particularly to pig production and beef rearing. These changes demand some very serious re-thinking about the subsidy system. Besides preventing the leakage of subsidies to outside interests, it is becoming more and more urgent to ensure that Government support goes to those who really need it.

Farmers rightly stress the immense value of the system of annual reviews and price guarantees, which provide the industry with some security and stability. But whilst retaining these basic provisions, it is worth considering whether the method of paying subsidies should be altered, particularly for those products which are being taken over by a few very large units, as in the case of eggs. Price guarantees are highly esteemed by farmers as a security against violent changes in farm incomes. But this security relates to three separate types of risk. There is the risk of natural hazards, including weather conditions and animal diseases, which are inherent in farming operations. There is the risk of market fluctuations, due to temporary gluts or shortages, which are also inseparable from primary production. There is, finally, the risk of undercutting by lower-cost imports, for which the guaranteed price provides a 'make-up' or deficiency payment to the farmer. The first two are really insurable risks, which could be covered by price insurance schemes. A stabilization fund could be set up for each commodity, to which farmers contributed when prices were high, and from which they drew payments when prices were low. The Government could provide funds to set the scheme going and give some guarantee of a minimum return in the event of an extreme or unexpected fall in price. It is possible that contributions could be levied on distributors and processors, since they have an interest in securing a stable and steady supply of the product. Schemes of this kind could also be used flexibly to lessen the inequality between large and small farmers, because contributions could be graded to the size of business or number of acres, and very small units could be exempted from contributions. In this way, the inequality in farmers' incomes could be lessened.

Some price subsidization would still be required for products with costs higher than those of imports, and this could be met either by a Government contribution to price stabilization schemes, or by separate deficiency payments. A gradual transition to partly self-supporting schemes of this type would promote a better understanding between farmers and non-farmers, and would enable the farming industry to win greater confidence and respect from the rest of the community. The case for expanding home production would be immeasurably strengthened.

Even if insurable farming risks were treated separately, a more fundamental question remains: should subsidization of prices continue indefinitely, or should this be tapered off over a period of years? It depends, first of all, upon how much food is going to be required in the next fifteen or twenty years. If world supplies were abundant, and very much less British food was needed, one possible policy would be the rapid abolition of subsidies. This would put thousands of less efficient farms out of business, and concentrate production in a few highly efficient units, occupying the best land. Other land would either go out of cultivation, or be amalgamated into larger units. This is the solution favoured by the 'restrictionist' group of economists. But all the signs suggest that very much *more* food is going to be needed in Britain, due to rising standards of living and rising population. The increase in demand for food might be as much as 30-40% by the end of the century. In these circumstances, it would seem exceedingly unwise to put land out of cultivation, to disperse skilled labour, or to cut down herds of livestock, since these productive resources, once lost, cannot be quickly restored. A more prudent course would be either to maintain agriculture at its present level or to plan for gradual expansion. If so, further time would be needed to improve the equipment and organization of the less efficient farms, and this would require some degree of price subsidization. But with productivity in the industry rising fast, and with economies in the marketing and handling of food, it seems likely that the proportion of subsidy could steadily decline, as it did in the case of milk, until no subsidy was required. But production grants would still be essential to encourage further capital improvements in land, buildings and equipment.

The amount of subsidy needed in the future depends also upon the cost of food in the shops. If the Government wanted food prices to be fixed even when the cost of other goods was rising, more subsidy would be needed. But in conditions where the majority of the population have rising incomes, it is open to doubt whether they require heavily subsidized food prices. The special needs of large families and old age pensioners could be met by higher children's allowances and pensions, while the price of food kept in step with that of other goods and services. With moderate subsidies and rising productivity on farms, food prices in Britain would still remain cheaper than the average throughout Europe.

The rate of subsidy must also be influenced by the standard of living that is considered appropriate for farmers, farm workers and their families. Over several generations, farm incomes in Britain were undercut by cheap food from abroad, much of it based upon cheap family labour. In the conditions of the 1960's, it seems unreasonable that the minimum farm wage should remain at £10 2s per week for an adult man, and that 40% of farmers should earn less than £600 a year. There is a certain parallel between farming and coal mining, since the coal industry was heavily run down before it was nationalized. Very large sums of capital have been required to bring the mines up to date, and a good many years elapsed before the Coal Board could show a surplus. But during this period of re-organization, the miners have not remained on the wretchedly low wages on which they existed before the war. Due to their strong trade union, they have established a high level of pay, related to their skill and to the tough and dangerous nature of the work. The rest of the community do not begrudge them these earnings. In the same way, farming is a highly skilled occupation, requiring great energy and effort in all weathers, and whilst the farming industry is in the process of being modernized, it seems reasonable that the men and women working in it should enjoy a standard of life comparable with that in other jobs.

The final decision on the amount of subsidy required is therefore exceedingly complex. There remain a number of unknown factors which will powerfully influence the decision. It is not easy to estimate for certain what is the future potential of British farming, in terms of total output, efficiency and costs, as compared with those of overseas suppliers. Farmers may tend to be too optimistic about this, and economists too pessimistic. It is even more difficult to estimate what are going to be the conditions of supply and demand for food on the international markets, in view of the rising world population, and the problem of poverty in the less developed countries. Yet these uncertain factors are vitally important to Britain's food supplies. It is these factors which will determine whether British farm production should be maintained at its present level, or whether it should be greatly expanded in the future. That is why, even with the limitations of incomplete knowledge, these factors are discussed in the following two sections.

PART II
BRITAIN'S FARMING POTENTIAL

CHAPTER 6

NATURAL RESOURCES

THE farming potential of a nation is made up of several components. It is based first of all upon the natural resources of land, soil, water and climate. If these are lacking, as in desert lands, then the development of agriculture is strictly limited. But besides natural resources, agriculture depends upon technical resources, which include the skill and experience of the labour force, the knowledge of crop and animal husbandry, machinery and equipment, buildings and services, and facilities for education and research. In addition, a farming industry needs what may be called economic resources, such as marketing organizations and access to capital and credit. These combined resources – natural, technical and economic – make up the farming potential of a nation at any given time.

The technical and economic resources may be fairly static, as in some peasant countries where conditions have remained stagnant for centuries, or they may be rapidly changing and developing, as in most parts of Europe today. The natural resources, too, may be enlarged or improved over much longer periods, by reclaiming land from the sea, as in Holland, or by works of irrigation, such as those which will be made possible by the Aswan High Dam in Egypt.

Many British citizens have no idea how rich their country is in natural resources for farming. Out of a total of about 60 million acres of land in the United Kingdom, 31 million are devoted to crops and grass, and another 17 million to rough grazing.

Use of Land in the United Kingdom[1]
Million Acres

	Total Area	Crops and Grass	Rough Grazing	Non-Farm Use	% Farm Use
England and Wales	37.1	24.4	5.0	7.7	79%
Northern Ireland	3.4	1.9	0.8	0.7	79%
Scotland	19.1	4.3	12.4	2.4	83%

[1] Ministry of Agriculture. Agricultural Statistics. U.K. 1961/62.

England and Wales have the highest proportion of crops and grass, whilst Scotland has a very high proportion of rough grazing due to the mountainous nature of the country. The proportion of land devoted to farming at around 80% is very high in the United Kingdom. In Australia, for example, only about 50% of the land is in agricultural use. In Europe, on the average 47% of the land is farmed, and in the USSR only 27%.[2]

The farming of 80% of the land in the United Kingdom is made possible by favourable climate and soil. According to Sir John Russell : –

'The United Kingdom is unusual in its wide range of natural conditions. It lies at the northern limit of the wheat belt of Europe, but the effect of the warm Atlantic winds is to allow the growth of plants that otherwise would be found only in more southerly climates. The effect is naturally most pronounced in the south-west and decreases in passing to the north-east : Cornwall and Devon can grow palms, grapes, and early vegetables, while north-east Scotland is so cold that aphids cannot thrive, in consequence potatoes escape the destructive aphid-borne virus diseases afflicting them in most of England; north-east Scotland thus became a reliable source of disease-free seed.'[3]

Rainfall varies from 30-60 inches per year over the greater part of the country, and is fairly evenly spread over winter and summer. The weather, which pre-occupies the British in conversation, and causes so much irritation to holidaymakers, is, in fact, exceedingly favourable for growing plants. The temperature varies between 40° and 60°F. for the greater part of the year, and outdoor activity can be carried on throughout the winter. On drier land, sheep and cattle can be kept out all the year round.

The soil, upon which farming depends, was created by a long process of natural development. When the Ice Ages ended, some 15,000 years ago, vegetation gradually spread in, and later dense forests covered the whole country for thousands of years. Prehistoric men cleared patches of forest, and this continued into Roman times. In the words of C. S. Orwin : 'Nearly all farmland

[2] FAO. *Production Year Book* 1962.
[3] Sir John Russell. *World Population and World Food Supplies*, p. 26. (Allen & Unwin, 1954.)

has been reclaimed at an infinite expenditure of manual labour from natural woodland.'[4] The forests gradually built up a layer of fertile soil. The colour, texture, and character of the soil varies from place to place, according to the nature of the underlying strata and rocks, the most important groups being the loams, the clays, and the chalklands, all of which can be highly productive under good management.

The system of farming practised in the Middle Ages, based on the three field rotation of winter wheat, spring corn, and fallow, was one which maintained the fertility of the soil. The enclosure movement, with the great increase in sheep farming, and later the new farming methods such as the Norfolk rotation of roots, barley, clover seeds, and wheat, with sheep being folded on the roots, added still more to the fertility of the land. The tradition of maintaining fertility is deeply ingrained in the minds of British and European farmers. Perhaps their high density of population has made them realize that their land is a heritage to be carefully guarded. This outlook and tradition, combined with the temperate climate, has preserved the greater part of British soil from the disaster of erosion – the loss of fertile soil by wind or water.

By contrast, the United States has suffered terrible losses from get-rich-quick systems of farming in conditions of severe rainfall in the east and scorching winds in the west. Professor Dudley Stamp reports : –

'It has been claimed that in the United States between 40-50% of the original fertility of the land has been lost since the First World War by water and wind erosion, over-cropping, and over-grazing.'[5]

The speed and extent of this destruction in a vast country with almost unlimited agricultural resources is truly horrifying. Where soil is partly eroded, new methods of cultivation and cropping can gradually restore it. But where erosion has worn the soil away, leaving only bare rock, it may be impossible to renew it. Conversely, where soil is preserved, its fertility is a natural resource which can go on being used for ever. Unlike coal mines,

[4] C. S. Orwin. *History of English Farming* (Nelson, 1952).
[5] Prof. Dudley Stamp. *Our Developing World*, p.78. (Faber, 1960.)

mineral deposits, or oil wells, fertile soil can be re-used and renewed indefinitely.

There is one part of the British Isles which has suffered heavily from erosion – this is the Highlands of Scotland. In the Middle Ages, more than 90% of Scotland was covered by forests, including oak, pine and larch. In a feature article entitled: 'Lost Forests of the Highlands', Richard Fitter describes the destruction of Scotland's greatest natural resource : –

'The vast area once covered with trees is now for the most part occupied by farmland at the lower levels and by heather and grass moorlands in the hills. What we think of as wild and natural in the Highlands, the bare outlines of the hills and the great purple sweeps of heather moorland, are in fact quite artificial, the product of centuries of abominably bad land management. Many of those who oppose the re-afforestation of the hill lands do not realize that the foresters are in fact doing no more than restore the status quo.'[6]

On the steeper hills and mountains, the forests absorbed the heavy rainfall and anchored the soil with their roots, whilst their falling leaves and branches renewed its fertility. When the forests were cut down, water rushed down the mountains, carrying away the fertile soil, turning rich and productive land into poor and barren moorland. In sharp contrast, Norway and Sweden, where forests have been preserved, have valuable timber industries, and thousands of farmers can earn additional income in forest work. Today, the world is using up timber resources at a great rate, for housing and furniture, and for the insatiable newspaper industry. In these circumstances, the restoration of forest in the Highlands of Scotland and parts of Wales would be a most valuable long-term investment, as well as bringing new life and work to remote areas.

Apart from the Highlands, temperate climate and fertile soil make possible a very wide range of farming activities in the United Kingdom. The eastern part of the country has a rainfall between 20-30 inches, well distributed over winter and summer, and this, combined with the good soils, provides excellent condi-

[6] Richard Fitter. *Observer*, May 6, 1962.

tions for corn crops and potatoes from East Anglia to Aberdeen, with sugar beet and field vegetables from Cambridge to Lincolnshire. The western half of the country, containing most of the hills and mountains, is correspondingly wetter and warmer, with rainfall varying from 30-60 inches. This land is very suitable for grassland farming, dairying, cattle and sheep, with early flowers and vegetables in the extreme south-west. Northern Ireland has a similar warm, moist climate, and has specialized in dairying and pig farming. The south of England and parts of the West Country are very suitable for horticulture. These varied conditions enable British agriculture to turn out a wide range of products. There is also some interdependence between the regions. The arable districts can produce fodder and straw for intensively kept livestock, while the grassland areas can maintain breeding herds of cattle and sheep, and rear young stock. The widespread practice of mixed farming, with crops and grazing animals using the land in rotation, maintains and increases the fertility of the soil.

The basic requirements for agriculture are:– good soil, sufficient rainfall, moderate temperatures and sunshine. The British Isles are very well supplied with the first three, but somewhat deficient in sunshine. This hinders the ripening of fruit and corn crops in unfavourable seasons. New Zealand has more sunshine, but in many areas the soils are relatively poor. In Australia, Canada and the western parts of the USA farming is limited by lack of rainfall. Extremely cold winters restrict farming activity for many months in northern Canada, and in the northern parts of the Soviet Union. High rainfall and intense humidity in the tropics hinder human activity, and cause heavy leaching of plant foods from the soil. In many parts of the Mediterranean, the soil has been impoverished by erosion, though sun and climate are favourable to plants. Very few countries in the world have perfect conditions for agriculture, and often the highly fertile regions are confined to one part of a country. The United Kingdom and other countries of north-western Europe have exceptionally favourable conditions for farming. These agricultural resources are one of our greatest national assets, which. if used rightly, can remain productive for all time.

CHAPTER 7

TECHNICAL RESOURCES

THE technical resources of agriculture may be defined as the means devised by men to obtain food and other useful products from natural resources. Technical resources include the accumulated skill and experience of farmers and farmworkers, and the facilities for agricultural education and research. They include, too, the stocks of farm animals and seeds, tools and machinery, fertilizers and chemical sprays, buildings and services. These resources have been created by many generations of effort. In the past, there have been several periods of rapid development in farming methods, including the second half of the eighteenth century, when the 'Norfolk Rotation' was introduced, and the period of 'high farming' between 1850-1880, but the developments of the last twenty-five years have been much faster and much more revolutionary than any that have occurred before. In all the industrially advanced countries, particularly in Europe, North America and Oceania, farming is being transformed from a small-scale handicraft occupation into a highly mechanized and capital intensive industry, based on scientific principles.

Britain is undoubtedly very rich in technical resources for agriculture. First and foremost is the labour force itself, which includes many highly skilled and experienced farmers and farmworkers, both men and women. They have an intimate knowledge of local soil and weather conditions, and the ability to handle livestock and machinery. Some farmers follow keenly the latest scientific discoveries, and technical methods, and apply them rapidly on their own farms. Others depend more upon practical experience, and are more cautious in adopting new methods until they have seen them in operation on other farms. Agricultural education is available at County Farm Institutes, which provide elementary courses, and Agricultural Colleges for more academic study. The facilities and training are of a high standard, and the living conditions for the students are usually very good. There is a lack of intermediate education to train high-grade technicians and foremen, capable of taking responsibility for a department, or an enterprise, on a farm. There is a shortage of these key men, and their training at present is left mainly to chance.

Britain has many well-known scientific institutions devoted to basic research in agriculture, including Rothamsted in Hertfordshire (soil and arable crops), East Malling in Kent (horticulture), Aberystwyth in Wales (grassland) and many others. These places are world-famous for their contribution to agricultural science. The practical applications of basic research are passed on to farmers by the National Agricultural Advisory Service, and by the advisers employed by private firms.

Britain has often been referred to as the stud farm of the world. So far as numbers and diversity of farm animals and poultry are concerned, this claim still has validity, but with the trend to large-scale production and distribution, the demand is for fewer breeds and strains with more uniform performance, based not upon appearance or show-ring points, but upon the production of high quality meat, milk or eggs. The Milk Marketing Board, by extensive recording and artificial insemination, has exerted a powerful influence on the leading dairy breeds. The Pig Industry Development Authority has set up Progeny Testing Stations, and is conducting statistical surveys of the various breeds of pigs In the Poultry Industry, a number of large private firms, employing geneticists, have succeeded in raising substantially the egg-laying capacity of pullets, and the meat-producing capacity of broiler chickens. But there is still a long way to go to sort out the immensely rich reservoir of genetical material in the various breeds and crosses, and to concentrate upon the types required by the market.

A supply of pure and reliable seeds for crops and grass is essential to efficient farming. These are supplied partly by specialized seed firms, and partly by local merchants. On the whole, standards are good, and stocks are continually being improved by the excellent work of plant breeders.

Farm machinery is, perhaps, the most outstanding of our technical resources. A large number of engineering firms have developed tractors, combine harvesters and countless machines and devices for mechanizing every conceivable farm job, with the result that British farms and horticultural holdings are among the most highly mechanized in the world. More than 400,000 tractors and 50,000 combine harvesters are in use. The very large export trade in farm machinery is an indication of its high quality.

Less visible, but equally essential, is the contribution of the chemical industry, with fertilizers to provide nitrogen, potash and superphosphate – the major plant foods. Without these, it would be impossible to obtain the high yields which are now common for corn, potatoes, grassland, sugar beet and other crops. Chemical sprays to control weeds and pests have also helped to raise production, but some of these have proved dangerous to wild life, and possibly to human life too, and it is necessary that more rigorous testing, over longer periods, should be enforced, when new materials are introduced.

The milling and compounding of animal feeding-stuffs is another key industry for farming. These firms buy the greater part of the home-grown cereal crop, and with the addition of imported cereals, fishmeal and the by-products from oil seed crushing, they prepare rations for cattle, pigs and poultry, which are very extensively used by farmers. These firms have large-scale plant and employ highly trained staff to carry out research on animal nutrition both in their laboratories and on their own farms.

The three major industries – farm machinery, chemicals, and feeding stuffs – are dominated by a few very large firms, which means that farmers, buying as individuals, have little or no bargaining power, and no means of negotiating on prices. While the goods supplied are generally of high quality, farmers cannot easily judge whether they are paying too much for them.

Finally, as the United Kingdom is so compact in size, and densely populated, public services including water, electricity, telephones and transport, are available in almost all districts, except the more mountainous parts of Scotland and Wales. These services are of immense value in raising efficiency and making farm life more pleasant and comfortable.

But there are several points at which our technical resources are deficient. Whilst the majority of farmers and workers are skilful and resourceful in carrying out everyday farming operations, the standard of management varies very widely between one farm and another. This is not surprising in view of the complexity of modern farming. Any one branch of livestock or crop husbandry requires great skill and experience, and as on most farms there are several enterprises, it requires first-class ability and knowledge to carry through an efficient farm plan. Further, the farm manager has to anticipate and allow for weather conditions, to recruit and handle labour, and to buy and sell economically. Farm managers possessing all these qualities are few and far between.

The most glaring weakness on British farms is the high proportion of obsolete and dilapidated farm buildings. These are a heritage from the long period of farming depression, when rents and farm incomes were so low that it was impossible either to repair them or replace them. Even those which are solidly built are more often than not inconvenient for handling livestock, and insufficiently warm and dry. Frequently, old buildings, intermixed with new ones, clutter up the yards and approaches to the farm, making the total layout awkward and time-wasting. As it is expensive to pull them down, attempts are often made to adapt them to present-day requirements, with only partial success. But many of the better-off farmers find that it pays them to scrap old buildings entirely, and start afresh.

Human beings in Britain have a National Health Service, but animals do not. Veterinary services are usually provided by groups of veterinary surgeons working in partnership and charging fees per visit and per treatment. Whilst many vets provide prompt and efficient service, at all hours of the day and night, the system does not adequately encourage the prevention of disease and the active promotion of animal health measures. Farmers do not normally call the vet until a cow or a pig is sick. Losses of young calves and baby pigs are still distressingly high. Mastitis and bloat give a lot of trouble in dairy herds. Parasitic infections are all too common in sheep, whilst many thousands of pigs are unthrifty due to enteritis and virus pneumonia. One of the greatest triumphs in animal health has been the complete eradication of tuberculosis from cattle in the United Kingdom. This was only possible by a national effort, directed by the Ministry of Agriculture. Similarly, the present attempt to eliminate entirely the disease of swine fever in pigs depends upon the enforcement of controls on the movement of animals, whenever the disease occurs, and the compulsory slaughter of affected herds. It is probable that a nationally organized veterinary service would more than pay for itself in terms of saving young animals and preventing disease.

In many countries, lack of technical resources severely hampers farm development. In the Soviet Union, for example, where land is abundant, and many excellent tractors and machines have been produced, the shortage of chemical fertilizers has held down the yields of crops, and the enlargement of the chemical industry to provide adequate fertilizers will require time and heavy investment. In thinly populated countries, as in Australia, public services which are taken for granted in Europe, cannot be provided for farms which are hundreds of miles from the nearest town, and this makes farming life much harder and lonelier, and encourages young people to leave the land. In the less developed countries, as in parts of Africa, lack of knowledge and training may result in appalling erosion of the soil, which aggravates the poverty of the people. By comparison, British farmers are exceedingly fortunate in having at their disposal all the major resources required for modern farming.

It is no easy task to compare the technical resources of one country with those of another. Good results may be partly influenced by soil and climate, whilst poor results may be due to social factors, such as an oppressive system of land ownership. Comparisons may be vitiated by unreliable statistics. The Food and Agriculture Organization of the United Nations, FAO, have made detailed studies of productivity in different countries, from which certain broad conclusions can be drawn. Farm productivity can be measured in a number of ways, of which the most significant are (i) productivity per unit of agricultural land, and (ii) productivity per man employed in agriculture.

Taking the use of land as a measure of efficiency, one or two examples indicate that the United Kingdom is amongst the group of countries obtaining the highest output from farm land. For wheat production, the highest average yields in the world, 32s cwt. per acre, are obtained in Western Europe, by the Netherlands, and Denmark, followed closely by the United Kingdom and Belgium. Outside Europe, average yields of more than 20 cwt. per acre are obtained only in New Zealand, Japan, and the United Arab Republic. In Australia and Canada, yields are limited by lack of rainfall to between $8\frac{1}{2}$-$10\frac{1}{2}$ cwt. per acre, or only about one third of those in Western Europe.[1]

In livestock production, milk yields are a convenient measure of productivity. Out of 42 countries, for the years 1958-60, the United Kingdom stood seventh. Israel and the Netherlands came first, followed by Belgium and Denmark.[2]

FAO make this comment : –

'More significant than either crop yields or livestock yields by themselves is the overall productivity of land, the whole output from each hectare of land used for agriculture. For while the individual yields reflect the efficiency of crop husbandry or live-stock husbandry, the overall productivity also takes into account the managerial skill with which the various farm enterprises are integrated to increase the total farm output.'[3]

By this measurement, out of 52 countries, the United Kingdom is placed eighteenth for the period 1956-60. Highest production of all is in the United Arab Republic, where in some irrigated areas three crops per year can be obtained. Other leading countries include those in north-west Europe, together with Formosa, Japan, Malaya and Ceylon. New Zealand and Canada – countries with more extensive systems of farming – are a fair way down the list, and Australia is at the bottom.[4]

When it comes to the productivity of labour, the order tends to be reversed, since the extensive systems use large amounts of land and machinery, with very few men. Taking the gross output per adult male worker for the period 1956-60, New Zealand, Australia, the USA and Canada come first, and next in order come Belgium, Denmark and the United Kingdom.[5] These statistics do not take account of unpaid family labour, which is very important in countries like Belgium, Denmark, and the Netherlands. If these unpaid workers are included as producers, calculations by the NFU show that Britain has the highest output per man in Europe. One man on a British farm produces enough food for 23 people. In Denmark. one farmworker can feed 17 people. In

---

[1] FAO. *Production Year Book* 1962.
[2] FAO. State of Food & Agriculture 1963, p. 108.
[3] FAO. *Ibid*, p.110.
[4] FAO. *Ibid*, p.110.
[5] FAO. *Ibid*, p.116.

West Germany the ratio is 1 to 9, in France 1 to 8, and in Italy 1 to 7.[6] According to FAO : –

'Undoubtedly, Denmark, the United Kingdom and the Netherlands should be credited with the highest level of agricultural labour productivity in Europe, and output per labour unit in these countries may be estimated to be 4-5 times greater than in Italy.'[7]

The surveys carried out by FAO provide an overall picture of productivity and technical resources in agriculture. It becomes clear that high productivity is at present obtained in three ways. First, there are those countries obtaining high productivity from land by intensive methods, using a large labour force, as in Japan, Formosa, the United Arab Republic, Ceylon and Malaya. At the other extreme, there are countries with high labour productivity, based upon extensive methods, using very large areas of land, combined with good machinery and skilful livestock husbandry, as in Australia, New Zealand, the Argentine, Canada and the USA. Finally, there are the countries of northwest Europe, including the United Kingdom, which combine both high labour output and an intensive use of land. Each of these three types of agriculture is contributing massively to the world's food supplies, and the choice of system is dictated partly by climate and soil, and partly by the technical resources available. So far as European farming is concerned, Britain is amongst the leading producers, and comes first of all in productivity of labour.

[6] NFU. 'Britain's Biggest Industry'. 1963.
[7] FAO. 'Towards a Capital Intensive Agriculture'. p. 40.

CHAPTER 8

ECONOMIC RESOURCES

GOOD land, and tools to work it – these are the first essentials for efficient farming. But to obtain maximum results, farmers are also dependent upon certain economic resources. The most important of these are : –

(i) The farming structure.
(ii) The supply of capital and credit.
(iii) Facilities for economical buying.
(iv) Sound marketing arrangements.

The farming structure, including the size and layout of farms, and the system of land tenure, has been determined in most countries by economic and political history, rather than by present-day farming requirements. The French Revolution, for example, established the peasants as a class of small proprietors, and the law of inheritance led to the fragmentation of holdings amongst the sons of later generations. In Britain, the growth of the wool trade stimulated the earliest enclosure movement in Tudor times, and gradually gave rise to a wealthy land-owning class. Between 1750-1850, the growth of industry and increased demand for food were accompanied by a rapid series of enclosures, replacing the mediaeval 'open fields' by a landlord and tenant system, depending upon hired wage workers. This agrarian revolution enabled Britain to become the most advanced agricultural country in the world by the middle of the nineteenth century. According to C. S. Orwin, high farming reached its peak between 1850-80 : –

'Never at any other time in its history has the land been better equipped by the landowner, better cultivated by the farmer, nor has food production from it been more intensive. Landlords and farmers collaborated in the means to good farming, secure from effective competition from overseas, and thus assured of good prices for everything which the land could produce. Only for the farmworker, unorganized, inarticulate and exploited, was the name "The Golden Age of British Farming" a bitter misnomer.[1]

The size and shape of British farms laid out in this period have remained without much change up to the present day. The average size of farm in England and Wales is 70 acres, compared with 25-40 acres in Denmark. In Italy, 93% of farm holdings are less than 25 acres.[2] Fragmentation of holdings, due to the feudal system of strip farming, is a most intractable problem in several European countries. According to Mr T. K. Warley: 'The typical German farm has 21.7 acres split into 11 separate pieces.'[3] The size structure in Britain, though superior to that of most European countries, is by no means ideal. Many farms are awkwardly shaped, and badly laid out. Some are split up by main roads or railways. There is at present strong pressure amongst the better-off farmers to acquire larger areas of land, either by amalgamating adjacent farms, or by operating several separate farms under one management. This trend is likely to continue.

Farming with modern methods requires a large amount of money, and the supply of capital and credit is of critical importance. There are several factors which make it more difficult to raise money for farming than for other industries. The hazards of weather and disease make it much more risky. The turnover of most farm products is relatively slow. Until recently, the majority of farms have been private businesses or partnerships, without the opportunity to raise capital on the Stock Exchange. Under the landlord and tenant system, it was the duty of the landlord to provide fixed capital for buildings, gates, drainage, roads and services, while the tenant had to supply livestock, machinery and working capital. So long as farming was prosperous, this system worked well, but the era of prolonged depression made farm land an unprofitable investment, and after half a

---

[1] C. S. Orwin. *A History of English Farming*, p. 73.
[2] Derek Healey. British Agriculture and the Common Market', p.7.
[3] T. K. Warley. Dept. Agric. Economics, Nottingham University. 'Impact of European Economic Integration on British Agriculture and the Commonwealth'.

century of neglect, it required a vast investment of capital to make good the arrears.

Production grants from the Government and the Farm Improvement Scheme have speeded up the job of re-equipment and renovation, but there is still a long way to go. Farmers themselves normally raise capital from private sources, including personal savings and help from relatives. They also make extensive use of bank credit when they can get it. Merchants' credits, hire purchase and advances on livestock from auctioneers provide additional resources at very high cost.

The minority of farmers, earning £3,000 per year or more, have no difficulty in obtaining the capital they require, either from banks or from businessmen who wish to invest funds in agricultural land. But the majority of small and medium farmers, earning from £600-1,800 per year in net farm income, have great difficulty in obtaining capital, particularly when they are not yet well-established. Owner occupiers can obtain long-term loans from the Agricultural Mortgage Corporation for two-thirds of the value of the property, but as their valuations are very conservative, the borrower may obtain only 50% of the actual purchase price of the farm. The Agricultural Credit Corporation was set up by the NFU, with the approval of the Government, to help farmers obtain more working capital, by giving additional guarantees for loans provided by the farmers' own banks. The Credit Corporation investigates the standing and efficiency of the farmer, and advises the bank accordingly. The snag in this arrangement is that the bank manager may interpret the farmer's position quite differently, and as the Credit Corporation cannot itself make loans, deadlock may ensue. A better alternative would be to set up a specialized Farm or Land Bank, with guarantees provided by the Government, with powers to lend to farmers on the security of land and stock. A bank of this kind would gradually build up a staff with expert knowledge of farming conditions and able to assess the soundness of farming enterprises. By enabling farmers to help themselves, a bank of this kind could save a lot of the money that is at present spent on farm subsidies.

As agriculture becomes more 'capital intensive', farmers tend to buy larger quantities of goods and services from other industries, and, in turn, have larger amounts of farm produce to sell.

Clearly, efficient buying and selling are essential, if the efforts devoted to production are not to be wasted. The traditional method was for the farmer to spend a day a week at the local market, where he could study the prices, hob-nob with his friends, and bargain with merchants and dealers. Some farmers still enjoy this weekly outing, but they are becoming fewer, because many farm products are sold direct to factories and processers, and because many farm requirements, such as machinery and feeding stuffs, are not available in markets. But it is not easy for farmers to buy on favourable terms, because most of their requirements – tractors, feed, fertilizers – are supplied by a few very large combines, normally dealing through local agents or merchants, with prices laid down at headquarters. With these giants, the individual farmer has no power to bargain. In this respect, the individualistic British farmer is worse off than his counterpart in Denmark, who has been accustomed for many years to buy and sell through co-operative organizations.

To remedy this weakness, farmers have started a number of buying groups in the last few years, through which orders can be bulked together, and valuable discounts obtained from manufacturers, ranging from 5-7% on building materials to 22% for tyres. Some of these groups operate autonomously, others are attached to County Branches of the NFU which may provide an office and a secretary, and others are organized by Agricultural Central Trading (ACT) – a national body set up by the Farmers Unions to stimulate the group movement, and to negotiate on a national scale with the manufacturers and suppliers. The conception of ACT is most ambitious: it is that this one super-buying agency should negotiate on behalf of farmers for the £950 million worth of goods and services which they buy from other industries. If supported 100% by farmers, the bargaining power of such a body would rival the largest government department.

But, as so often happens in Britain, these bodies have grown up haphazardly, and in some districts they are at loggerheads with one another. The traditional Farmers Co-operatives, supplying a full range of services, have also been expanding rapidly, and improving their facilities, and there has been some bad feeling between them and the buying groups on the grounds that the groups are diverting business from the co-operatives. But in spite of this confusion and friction, a cardinal principle has been

74

grasped by farmers, that so far as buying is concerned, unity is strength. So long as several hundred thousand separate farmers buy in penny packets, they will pay dearly. Up to now, the majority of farmers have in reality been buying at retail prices whilst selling at wholesale prices.

Marketing is undoubtedly the weakest link in the economic resources of British farming. Only a few products are marketed economically and efficiently. These include milk and wool, which are handled entirely by National Marketing Boards. Transport and distribution can be rationalized, and prices are fixed at the Annual Price Review. All sugar beet is purchased by the British Sugar Corporation, at guaranteed prices related to sugar content, and the crop is despatched direct from the farm to the nearest Corporation factory. For these products, the farmer has no marketing worries, and he knows what price to expect, according to the quality of his output.

But the marketing of many other farm commodities is costly, wasteful and inefficient. As the majority of the population live in urban areas and large cities, the chain of distribution has become longer and more complicated. For example, sheep, cattle and pigs may be transported from the farm to the local market, purchased by dealers, resold in other markets, then conveyed to a slaughterhouse, and from there to a wholesaler, ending up finally in a retail butcher's shop. These roundabout methods subject the animals to unnecessary suffering, and prevent high standards of hygiene. The costs of distribution are multiplied. Figures collected by the Verdon Smith Committee on meat marketing showed that processing and distribution of meat added 83% to the cost at the farm gate and at the docks. Commenting on the handling of meat, Professor Crossley writes : –

'. . . the meat trade is almost mediaeval. To a large number of farmers rearing animals is added a large number of butchers cutting up carcases in thousands of shops. In addition, the bones (which comprise about 25% of the total weight) are transported about the country and even sold to the consumer, who does not want them, merely because they happen to be inside the meat.

'Undoubtedly, much of this handling of carcases will be transferred to centralized meat factories, where mechanical aids to efficiency can be employed. From these factories, meat will be distributed in boneless form, probably deep frozen, and wrapped in portions for sale in self-service shops."[4]

As far as fruit and vegetables are concerned, the wide gap between growers' prices and shop prices has often baffled and angered the public, when they read of lettuces being ploughed in at the same time as they are selling at 1s 6d each in the shops. A high proportion of horticultural produce is sold on commission in wholesale markets in the big cities. Selling is not by grade or sample, and thus the whole consignment must be taken into a heavily congested market, such as Covent Garden in London, unloaded, displayed, and reloaded. Vegetables grown in Bedfordshire may pass through Covent Garden, and be brought back for sale to towns in Hertfordshire and Buckinghamshire, only ten or twenty miles from their starting point. This chaotic non-system is extremely wasteful economically, and pushes up prices in the local shops.

Many of these methods of distribution are a hangover from the past, when every farmer's wife took eggs, butter and poultry to the local market, and bargained direct with the housewife. For localized transactions, markets can still provide a useful service, as they can for the purchase and sale of store animals. But for the large-scale supply of food to big cities, much of the system is outdated. Farmers themselves have for many years tried to obtain better returns by organizing co-operatively owned packing stations for eggs, poultry, fruit and vegetables, which endeavour to sell direct to shops, hotels and institutions. Some of these enterprises have been very successful, and the Government has made grants available to assist new co-operative packing stations, and to improve the facilities for cold storage, cooling, packing and grading at existing stations. At the same time, a number of private firms have been rationalizing the procurement of their supplies. Several large meat handling concerns buy pigs and cattle direct from farmers through local agents, by-passing the markets, and transport the stock straight to their own abbatoirs and processing factories. In Lincolnshire, a giant prepacking plant is being built by a firm which distributes both home and imported fruit and vegetables to 300 stores and 450 supermarkets. They

[4] Prof. Crossley. *Journal of the Association of Agriculture*. July 1963.

plan to turn out 10 million prepacks per week, despatched by nightly trunk lorries to eleven distributing centres. It is claimed that vegetables growing in Lincolnshire fields one day will be on supermarket counters on the other side of the country by nine o'clock the following morning.[5] Farmers will be encouraged to produce on contract to specified standards. and to send regular consignments. Organizationally, this system will be far more efficient and economical than the traditional channels of distribution.

But these new developments have dangerous implications for the farmer. He may find that he has struggled out of the frying pan into the fire: that he has escaped the exploitation of the big wholesale markets only to become the slave of the big processing plants. It would appear essential for farmers and growers to be well-organized in local groups supplying a particular product, so that they can negotiate on the terms of the contract. If farmers try to bargain individually, they could find themselves worse off than under the old system, even though the public might be getting a much better service. The danger of monopoly control is also showing itself in farm production. This is illustrated by the plan of one producer to capture 20% of the egg market, by establishing battery units for 8 million birds. Two or three units of this kind, backed by large-scale capital from outside farming, could abolish entirely the conditions of free competition, and would reduce the Egg Marketing Board to impotence.

Recently, the Government has placed stronger emphasis upon improved marketing, grading and packing of farm produce by setting up the Agricultural Marketing Development Executive Committee (AMDEC). This body has funds to promote new marketing groups, to pay salaries for full-time managers, whilst groups are getting on their feet, and to conduct marketing research. This encouragement to better marketing, though valuable, is hardly adequate to the situation. The rapid growth of supermarkets and large processing firms means that within the next five to ten years food distribution will be dominated by a few very large firms, with a monopolistic influence on prices. British farmers will also continue to work at a disadvantage compared with their foreign competitors. All the major food exporting countries have market-

[5] Report in *Farmers Weekly*, June 5, 1964.

ing organizations to grade, sell and advertise their products – Danish bacon, New Zealand lamb, Argentine beef. In order to hold their own, British products will have to attain higher standards of quality, which will need to be publicised and promoted. As exports of pedigree livestock, seeds and other farm products continue to grow, these, too, need to be advertised and encouraged by an organization with sufficient funds and expert staff. At present, this task is left to the efforts of a few enthusiastic individuals. For these several reasons, food marketing and distribution require more government control and supervision, in order to safeguard the interests of both producers and consumers. There is a strong case for National Commodity Commissions, particularly for meat and grain, to co-ordinate imports with home production, to ensure reasonable prices, and to promote efficient and hygienic methods of handling. It is quite certain that if things are left to chance, there will continue to be waste, muddle and exploitation.

CHAPTER 9

HOW MUCH COULD BRITAIN PRODUCE?

THE farming industry has within itself a great potential for expansion, and by comparison with many other countries our farming resources are very diverse and very rich. If more food was needed, either due to rising population or due to shortage of imported supplies, it would be necessary to assess rather more accurately how much could be produced at home. At present, British agriculture is supplying about 66% of our temperate foodstuffs. In the event of need, could this proportion be raised to 80%, 90% or 100%?

Even without adding anything to existing farm resources, there is scope for a very substantial increase in food production. This is possible because of the very wide range of efficiency between the best and worst operators. Some of these variations arise inevitably from natural conditions. The soil may be poor, or the farm may occupy a cold and exposed position. Remoteness from markets or lack of electricity and water supply may limit the type of farming that can be carried on. But even on farms with similar land, the variations in performance persist, and run right through all the sizes of farm, from the under 50 acre group to the over 500 acre group. The annual statistics collected by the Ministry of Agriculture show that there are very large farms making a loss or only £5 per acre net profit, and there are medium and small farms making £20-25 per acre.

In some cases, low levels of efficiency are due to lack of capital, compelling the farmer to use unsuitable buildings and inadequate machinery, and restricting his working capital, so that he cannot raise his output to a point that uses the labour on the farm most effectively. This situation is very common on the medium and smaller farms. As their financial results are poor, they cannot easily obtain additional capital from the bank. Some of these farms subsist for long periods in a vicious circle of low credit, low efficiency and low income. So far as production is concerned, their output is usually well below the inherent capacity of the farm.

At the other end of the scale, there are farmers with a large acreage of land who by personal choice are operating well below the maximum potential of the farm. If a man has 800-1,000 acres, particularly if it is good arable land, he will make a very comfortable living even at £5 an acre net profit, bearing in mind that the farm provides him with a house, a car and many other amenities as part of his business expenses. He could make a higher profit by farming more intensively and adding one or more livestock enterprises, but this would bring additional worry and labour problems, not to mention supertax, and he may prefer instead to increase his leisure, taking more time off for hunting, shooting, farm shows or holidays. This trend has been encouraged by the present distribution of subsidies which have been exceptionally favourable to farmers with 200 acres or more of corn crops.

Even when the farmer is eager to earn as much as possible, and when land is good and capital available, there are still wide variations in results on comparable farms. In these cases, the decisive factor is the managerial ability of the farmer. A very high level of knowledge, experience and determination is required to manage a farm successfully, and in practice the standards vary enormously, from the supreme to the abysmal.

Clearly, to level up the less efficient to the standards of the leading producers would raise total output very considerably. To some extent, this is happening all the time, because the industry is in a state of change and transition.

Besides levelling up the inefficient producers, the farming industry is expanding production through the application of new techniques and methods. The mechanization of more and more operations has been raising the productivity of labour by 5% per annum, and this is expected to increase to 6½% per annum in the next few years. Many devices have been invented for moving dung, feeding animals, lifting and stacking straw bales, handling silage etc. Bulk milk tanks are replacing heavy milk churns. Grain and feeding stuffs can be handled in bulk from silos or hoppers into specially equipped lorries, eliminating the laborious job of sack-lifting. Experiments have been going on for some time with remote-controlled tractors, which plough or cultivate the fields unattended!

The yields of corn crops have risen dramatically in the last twenty-five years, from 18 cwt. per acre average for wheat in 1938 to 29½ cwt. today. On the better soils, this average is easily surpassed by the more skilful farmers, yields of 35-40 cwt. being quite common. In isolated cases, yields of 45 cwt., 50 cwt. and even 60 cwt. have been reported from time to time. There is every reason to expect that yields will be raised further in the next ten or fifteen years, since new machinery, better fertilizers and more prolific varieties are being developed all the time. In the drier eastern half of the country, irrigation systems are being adopted, and are raising the yields of potatoes, vegetables and sugar beet. There are also various systems of organic irrigation, whereby the sewage from intensive pig or cattle units can be pumped on to the land through pipe-lines or from special tankers, building up the fertility of the soil. In the production of barley, Britain is largely self-supporting, and increased production might displace some of the imported maize which is used for animal feeding stuffs. In the case of wheat, with imports accounting for 63% of the supply, even a very substantial increase in yields would not make us self-supporting, unless a lot more land were devoted to the crop. The use of more home-grown wheat for bread-making would depend upon the success of the plant breeders in developing high-yielding varieties for this purpose, suited to our damp climate.

The dairy industry has shown a steady rise in average milk yields per cow over the last twenty-five years, from 540 gallons per cow to 636 gallons. Amongst the leading producers, yields of 800-900 gallons are achieved with economical feeding based mainly on grass and grass products, and 1,000-1,200 gallons with more expensive concentrate feeding. The A.I. Service provided by the Milk Marketing Board has made possible very large-scale breeding operations, which are helping to raise milk yields. The science and practice of grassland management has also advanced greatly, making possible much higher returns per acre in hay, silage or grazing.

But many dairy farmers find themselves under heavy pressure of rising costs, and in recent years thousands have been giving up. partly due to low income and partly due to the long hours

F   81

and the exacting nature of the work. As no subsidy is paid, their income cannot be raised except by putting up the price of milk to the consumer, which vote-conscious Governments are reluctant to do. With so many dairy farmers giving up, the immediate prospect is a slowing down in growth, although the herds that remain tend to have more cows. As the demand for milk is rising, there is the possibility of shortage.

There is a much greater chance of expansion in meat production. The new intensive systems of keeping poultry, pigs and beef cattle have made possible very great increases in output. By providing convenient and comfortable buildings, and by mechanizing the handling of food and the removal of dung, a highly skilled stockman can look after 80-100 sows, or 400 beef cattle. Instead of humping sacks or shovelling muck, he can devote his attention to improving the health, nutrition and breeding of the animals. Where these systems are well organized, they can result in a very high output per unit of labour, and a very high level of performance from the stock.

These methods were applied first to poultry, for the production of eggs and table birds. Excessively rapid expansion led to a number of disastrous slumps, and failure to apply strict hygiene caused some very serious outbreaks of disease. But, in spite of these defects, the system has enabled home producers to supply all our requirements of eggs and chickens. For eggs, the subsidy has been declining, and for broilers there has been no subsidy from the start.

The intensive system is also being applied to pig production, but as most pigs are kept on general farms, it is being brought in more cautiously and carefully, with moderate-sized units, on which disease can be kept in check. Some of the very large pig units have had severe outbreaks of swine fever.

The latest form of intensive production is for 'barley beef' – the rearing of beef cattle in yards or stalls on a concentrated diet, consisting mainly of barley, and selling at about one year old, instead of the traditional two to three years old. This system is still in the experimental stages, and problems of disease and housing have yet to be resolved. But it seems likely that, as with pigs and poultry, it will make possible a big expansion of beef production at moderate cost. Some producers are continuing with semi-intensive methods, grazing the cattle for one or two summers, and feeding silage plus concentrates in yards during the winter. These animals can be finished at about 1½ years. With the world shortage of beef, it is probable that all systems of beef rearing will be improved.

The intensive systems of keeping livestock represent a new stage in animal husbandry, making possible more regular deliveries of more uniform products than in the past. The slaughter of young immature animals and poultry inevitably leads to some loss of flavour, but this is in accord with present-day tastes, particularly among the younger people. These systems make possible very large-scale production of chicken, pork and beef at prices which the ordinary family can afford, and this can be beneficial in a country where land is as scarce as it is in Britain.

There is some fear that intensive units will become vast inhuman animal factories, in which the livestock will suffer distress. In the experimental stages, there are likely to be some abuses, and problems of disease, hygiene and stress have arisen. When more experience has been gained, it may be necessary to lay down minimum legal standards for these enterprises, both for the animals and for the men and women who look after them. Those who violently oppose intensive systems on principle are inclined to forget that traditional methods of keeping livestock were by no means ideal. Many calves died in cold draughty loose-boxes. In the muddy hen-run, the birds were often wet and bedraggled, and their eggs heavily caked with muck. Outdoor pigkeeping, which is splendid in dry weather, can be a wretched existence for pigs and stockmen in November and December. The new methods, if used wisely, can provide better conditions for both workers and animals.

Even if the intensive systems are widely adopted, many millions of sheep and cattle will need to be kept outdoors, to supply breeding-stock and young store animals. To expand these herds would require more good grazing land. This is not easy because the United Kingdom has no large areas of rich farmland lying idle and waiting to be colonized. There are a few coastal regions which might be reclaimed from the sea, for example, the Solway Firth, the Wash and Morecambe Bay. But by far the largest areas of land suitable for improvement and reclamation are in the hills – in Wales, the Pennines and the Scottish Highlands. Dr William Davies, Director of the Grassland Research Station at Hursley, told the British Association in 1960:–

'We have within our shores a large, completely underdeveloped countryside – 17 million acres of it, lying chiefly above the 800 ft. contour. Upwards of 10 million acres of that land are on easy undulating slopes and are readily tractable.'[1]

A number of pioneering individuals continue to persevere with reclamation and improvement, which, though costly at first, provides them with valuable new acres when completed, at prices comparable with those now being paid for lowland farms. But this work requires so much capital that it is difficult, if not impossible, for the average hill farmer to undertake. If a great increase in meat supplies was needed, it might be necessary for the Government to undertake reclamation, combined with forestry, over large areas, and at the same time re-organize some of the farms into larger units, with provision for housing the stock in winter, and with better social facilities for the families living on them.

With these improvements, the hill lands could support many more sheep and cattle. If winter housing was available, the risks and losses of a hard winter would be lessened. The hills could provide the reserves of store sheep and cattle which are needed for fattening and finishing on lowland farms, as well as doing some fattening themselves. Improved methods of marketing, which enabled hill farmers to supply stock on contract at fixed prices, could make the job less speculative. The prospect of earning a fair income, with reasonable living conditions, would attract some of the pioneering and adventurous young couples, who at present often decide to emigrate.

These changes in hill farming would require, at first, a very large amount of capital, from the Government and from farmers. In the long run, costs would compare favourably with those of other parts of Europe, or with countries like Australia where production is limited by drought. New Zealand costs would probably remain lower, due to their favourable climate and easier winters, but the British producers should increasingly

[1] *Farmer and Stockbreeder*, Sept. 6, 1960.

84

benefit from proximity to the markets. The valuable export of British wool, and the small export trade in lamb to the continent, could be increased.

This brief survey indicates that Britain has an immense farming potential for the future. The Nuffield Foundation published in 1960 a study of British Agriculture, in which they estimated that :–

'. . . a combination of ley farming, together with the general application of the best-known agricultural methods, could increase agricultural output by up to £500 million a year, or rather more than 35% above recent levels.'[2]

This estimate was based upon figures collected in the 1950's, and more recent developments in crop yields and intensive systems of livestock suggest that the estimate may be too low. The NEDC calculate that between 1961-66 farm output will rise by about 18%, or 3.3% per annum. It is also estimated that due to rising population and higher incomes consumption of food will rise by 2% per annum.[3] If these trends continued, home production would provide for the increased demand for food, and would make us 75-80% self-supporting in temperate foodstuffs by 1975. These growth rates are taking place in spite of the squeeze on farmers' incomes, the exceptional difficulties experienced by dairy farmers, and the weakness of many hill farming enterprises. If expansion was actively promoted by the Government, the growth rate could be much greater.

But expansion cannot be considered apart from costs. and particularly the relative costs of imported supplies. In the past, importers have been able to undercut the British producer by a wide margin, and this has influenced Governments to restrict home output. But the overall prospect is now more favourable for British agriculture, with the probability that overseas costs will rise faster than our own.

Britain is most likely to compete successfully in grain production. In Canada and Australia, yields of grain are limited by lack of rainfall to only about one third of those in Britain, so that they

---

[2] Nuffield Foundation. *Principles for British Agricultural Policy*. Edited by H. T. Williams, p.197. (Oxford University Press, 1960.)

[3] NFU. 'British Agriculture Looks Ahead', p. 23-24.

cannot offset rising costs of machinery or labour by growing more per acre. During 1964, Canadian wheat was coming into Britain at £29-30 per ton.[1] In Britain, between 1961-1964 the standard price for wheat has been about £26 per ton, and for 1965 it has been reduced to £25 10s. In the Common Market, wheat prices are very much higher, the guide price in France being about £30 10s and in Germany over £37! British growers are still receiving a subsidy, but this will tend to fall as higher world prices increase the market realization for wheat in Britain. It is clear that in grain growing, Britain is already one of the most economical and efficient producers.

Next to grain, British farmers are most likely to hold their own in meat production. The producers of broiler chickens are supplying the whole of our requirements without subsidy. In pork production too, Britain is practically 100% self-supporting. A subsidy is paid on pork, varying from about 30s per pig to nil at different times of the year, according to the state of the market. The quality of fresh pork has been improving, and it is becoming a popular choice at all times of the year. The retail price is lower than in other countries in Western Europe.

British beef, which is sold fresh, is generally preferred to chilled Argentine beef. At the moment, the prices are comparable, except for genuine Scottish beef, which is more expensive as a luxury item. Beef cattle receive a subsidy, but in recent years higher market returns have at certain times of the year reduced the subsidy to nil for limited periods. Subsidies on cattle fell from £46½ million in 1961-63 to £12¾ million (forecast) for 1964/65.[5]

The Argentine producers rely upon extensive production on grassland, most of which is unimproved. Britain is better supplied with technical resources, both for improving grassland and for setting up intensive units. It seems likely, therefore, that home-produced beef will continue to compete strongly, with a declining rate of subsidy. Although the retail price is higher than it was a few years ago, it is still considerably lower than in most other European countries.

In the case of bacon, 64% of the total is imported from a

[1] Commonwealth Economic Committee Grain Bulletins.
[5] *Annual Review* 1965. **Cmd.** 2621.

number of countries, including Holland, Eire, Poland and Sweden, with Denmark being by far the largest supplier. Danish bacon normally sells for a higher price than equivalent grades of English. It is able to command this premium because of its consistently high quality, in comparison with the British product which is still too variable. Bacon pigs in Britain receive a subsidy, and since 1961 farm subsidies have also been paid in Denmark, to reduce fertilizer prices, to assist small farms, and to improve marketing. In 1962, domestic prices in Denmark for beef, veal, poultry-meat and eggs were raised above export prices, so that in effect the Danish consumer is subsidizing the exports of food to Britain and elsewhere. Allowing for the subsidies in both countries, there is not a lot of difference in costs and prices between English and Danish bacon. The problem for the British farmer is one of quality, rather than cost, and this is gradually being tackled by the County Quality Bacon Associations.

For several years milk has been produced without any subsidy. Retail prices in Britain are slightly higher than those in Europe, but, as mentioned earlier, the standards of hygiene and the delivery service are superior. Cheap milk in Denmark, Holland, France and other neighbouring countries is dependent upon cheap family labour, and as industrial production increases the younger people are leaving the farms. Sooner or later, costs in these countries will rise to somewhere near the British level, or even higher.

At present, we import 89% of our butter and 54% of our cheese. If more home-produced supplies were needed, the dairy industry would have to be expanded further, by the intensive use of grass and grass products, and there would have to be a more favourable price for manufacturing milk. There are no subsidies on British butter or cheese, and retail prices are lower than those of Holland and Denmark, but slightly higher than those of New Zealand. The crisis of costs and incomes, which is at present causing great anxiety amongst dairy farmers, makes it difficult to forecast future trends.

The examples given suggest that farm costs in the United Kingdom are becoming more competitive. British costs are being reduced, or held steady, by rapidly rising productivity, whilst the costs of overseas suppliers are tending to rise. Only New Zealand still retains a big cost advantage in butter and fat lamb production, due to their favourable climate and high level of technical efficiency. Even there, costs might rise if their farmers, who work intensely hard, began to demand a higher standard of living. The long-term prospect for Britain is hopeful, and so far as foreign competition is concerned, the need for subsidies is likely to decline.

So far, the price of food has been considered only from the aspect of *costs of production*. But world prices are, of course, also influenced by the *demand for food* on the international markets. Hitherto, Britain has been the largest food buyer in the world, with suppliers vying with each other for the trade. But in the future, this situation may be changed. Some of the primary producers, including the Argentine and Australia, need more food for their own consumption, and have less to spare for export. Furthermore, new food buyers are appearing, who are competing for world supplies. These include Japan, the Soviet Union and China, and may later include countries like India, which are densely populated and deficient in food supplies. The effect could be to raise the price of New Zealand lamb, Canadian wheat and Argentine beef, and to make it harder for Britain to obtain the required quantities. Changes of this kind would, therefore, influence the comparative prices of British and overseas food supplies. In the long run, it is these world developments which will determine how far Britain should use the great farming potential that has been outlined, and, if it is to be developed, how soon expansion should be put in hand.

PART III

WORLD POPULATION AND WORLD FOOD SUPPLIES

CHAPTER 10

THE THREAT OF WORLD HUNGER

THERE has emerged within the last hundred years a new and alarming problem for humanity – 'the population explosion'. Whereas, over several thousand years, the human race evolved slowly and painfully from the jungle, reduced often by famine, cold and disease, the economic developments of the last century have been accompanied by an accelerating growth of population on a scale never known before. At the time of Christ's birth, it is believed that there were about 200-300 million people in existence. This number crept up slowly through the era of feudalism to about 500 million by the seventeenth century. The rate of growth increased in the next 200 years, coinciding with the spread of trade and the beginnings of industry, and by 1850 world population had reached about 1,000 million. But by 1960, just 110 years later, this total had leaped to 3,000 million – 3 times the 1850 figure. For the next 40 years, the prospect is one of fantastic growth. If present trends continue, world population would *double again* by the year 2000, reaching about 6,000 million people.[1]

This mighty outburst of new life could mean a great accumulation of talent, skill and energy for the many tasks which await man's attention. But it could also bring in an age of starvation and misery unparalleled in human history. Quite simply, it depends whether the present generation of men and women can organize a sufficient food supply for the multitudes which are to be born. The problem is so vast, and so near at hand, that no thinking person can ignore it. The implications for Britain are particularly serious, in view of our dependence upon world food supplies.

The immediate outlook is bleak. Only about 29% of the world's

[1] FAO. 'Population & Food Supply', p.1-3.

people live in economically developed regions, in Europe, the USSR, North America and Oceania, but these areas produce 57% of the world's food supplies. By contrast, 71% of the people, living in less developed countries in the Far East, Near East, Africa and Latin America, produce only 43% of the food supplies.[2] According to FAO:– 'Diets of the mass of the people in the less developed regions remain appallingly low.'[3] It is in these regions that population is growing fastest, and agricultural methods are primitive.

Hunger is divided, in medical terms, into two categories – undernutrition and malnutrition. Undernutrition means that the diet is inadequate in quantity in terms of calories, allowing for slightly different requirements in different parts of the world due to the climate and the stature of the people. The effects of undernutrition are loss of weight and reduced physical activity in adults, and retarded growth in children. Malnutrition means that the diet is inadequate in quality, in particular that it is lacking in protein, vitamins and minerals. The effects of malnutrition are poor general health, and deficiency diseases. In practice, undernutrition and malnutrition usually go together.

Britain is among the fortunate minority of countries in which most people are well fed, and few are hungry. From this secure and comfortable island, it is hard to imagine the effects of hunger and starvation upon people in the underdeveloped countries. The most serious defects in diet arise from lack of animal and vegetable protein, and lack of green and yellow vegetables and fruits. In some areas these foods are not available, in others religious taboos, ignorance and wrong methods of cooking deprive people of the benefit of such supplies as are to hand. The general effects of poor diet are listlessness and lack of energy, poor physical development, low resistance to infections and disease, and low expectation of life. Infant mortality, which in the advanced countries is below 40 per 1,000, reaches 100 per 1,000 in Asia and Latin America, and even 200 per 1,000 in parts of Africa.[4] In countries where children are weaned on to a starchy diet, based upon maize, yams, or cassava roots, they are often attacked by

[2] FAO. 'Third World Food Survey 1963, Table 9.
[3] FAO. *Ibid*, p.20.
[4] FAO. *Ibid*, p.2.

the terrible disease of kwashiorkor, which damages the liver, and leads to odema and wasting, with outbreaks of sores. This disease may prove fatal. Lack of vitamin A can cause total and incurable blindness, as well as skin disorders. This trouble is widespread in Indonesia, Burma and the semi-arid zones of Africa. On the west coast of Africa, however, where red palm oil, rich in vitamin A, is used, this disorder is rare. Lack of vitamin B, where highly polished rice is used, can give rise to sore lips and tongues, and the disease of beri-beri. Iron deficiency leads to nutritional anaemia, particularly serious for mothers and babies, and lack of calcium gives rise to rickets, even in some hot countries.[5] Pellagra, arising from a maize diet, can lead to insanity.[6] These dreadful diseases and afflictions are entirely preventable if a full and balanced diet is available.

The reality of starvation is made clear by an account in *The Guardian* in August 1963 of crop failure in the North Transvaal in South Africa. According to their correspondent : –

'It is not generally known what the true state of affairs is in Vendaland. After more than 2 years of serious drought, a general food shortage has arisen in virtually the whole area north of Pietersberg . . . children are starving to death. In the past few months, 9 children under 5 have died of kwashiorkor here, and pellagra is rife.'[7]

The correspondent adds further details : –

'. . . 301 cases of kwashiorkor and 1,224 of pellagra treated in five hospitals in two districts alone between September 1962, and February 1963, apart from many more cases left untreated in the villages; hundreds of thousands of people already reduced to three meals of thin mealie porridge a week; the countryside swept bare of the wild spinaches normally used to supplement the diet; no prospect of relief from a new harvest before February or March 1964.'[7]

[5] FAO. *Ibid*, p.45.
[6] Dr Norman Wright 'Hunger – Can it be Averted', p.5-6 (British Association).
[7] *The Guardian*, August 9, 1963.

Apart from the appalling toll of physical suffering, hunger and malnutrition have insidious effects upon mental outlook and capacity. Dr Norman Wright, Deputy Director of FAO, comments as follows :–

'Observations in countries where there have been degrees of undernutrition, varying from severe, through temporary food shortages (as in the two world wars) to semi-starvation (as in many natural famines) indicate that under such conditions there is not only weight loss and reduction in physical activity, but also characteristic behaviour symptoms such as lack of mental alertness and coherent and creative thinking, apathy, depression and irritability, leading in extreme instances to an increasing loss of moral standards and social ties.'[8]

The stark fact must be faced: that men and women become undermined, physically and mentally, by starvation, and are deprived of the very qualities which are essential to overcome their plight. To arrange emergency relief, to set in motion plans for the next harvest, to improve agricultural methods – all this requires energy, initiative, drive, self-sacrifice and co-operation. Yet it is these abilities which are eroded away by prolonged periods of starvation. It becomes harder and harder for people to help themselves. According to FAO :– '. . . low incomes, low food consumption and low productivity thus go together in a "circle of poverty" which is still common to nearly all the less developed countries.'[9]

It would be a mistake to suppose that food shortages occur only in remote rural areas. There has been in recent decades a very rapid growth of cities, and today about 500 million people live in urban areas of 20,000 people or more.[10] In the advanced industrial countries, workers are drawn to the big cities to work in factories, docks and commerce, and complex systems of food distribution exist. In Italy, thousands are leaving Sicily and the south for the industrial areas of the north. But in many less developed countries, when rural workers desert the countryside and come to the cities looking for jobs, they find either that jobs

[8] Dr Norman Wright. 'Hunger – Can it be Averted', p.3-4.
[9] FAO. Third World Food Survey 1963, p.26.
[10] FAO. Population and Food Supply, p.19.

do not exist, or that they are debarred from getting work by illiteracy and lack of skill. These workers and their families exist in shanty towns on the outskirts of great cities, as in parts of South America. Their presence may aggravate the food shortage, because to feed people in cities more transport is needed to bring food from rural aras, and there must be facilities for storing and preserving the supplies.

Summing up the world food situation, FAO conclude : –

'. . . some 60% of the people in the underdeveloped areas, comprising some *two thirds* of the world's population, suffer from malnutrition or undernutrition or both.
'Since there are undoubtedly some people in the developed countries who are also ill fed, it is concluded that *up to half of the people in the world are hungry or malnourished.'*[11]

There are two ways in which the vast problem of hunger can be met. One is by efforts to moderate the rate of growth of population, the other is by efforts to raise food supplies. The control of population seems, at present, to offer the greater difficulty, because not enough is known about the causes of population growth, nor the circumstances in which growth might slow down. In Western Europe, North America and the USSR rapid population growth accompanied industrial development, which greatly increased the national wealth, and at the same time raised the productivity of agriculture. In each of these regions, rising standards of life sooner or later gave rise to a conscious desire for smaller families, and limitation was made possible by the spread of birth control. Improved health services have gone on lowering the death rate, so that populations are still growing, and the rate of growth, though slower than at the end of the nineteenth century, is considerably faster than in earlier times. These changes in birth and death rates are referred to as 'the demographic revolution'.

The experience of Japan has been similar to that of other industrial countries, but telescoped into a much shorter period. In 1951, an intensive campaign for birth control was started, and it is believed that about half the married couples now use

---

[11] FAO. Third World Food Survey 1963, p.51.

contraceptives. In addition, abortion was legalized and encouraged. Between 1950-60, the birth-rate was halved, but the death-rate dropped from the pre-war figure of 17.4 per 1,000 to 7.4 per 1,000, and the expectation of life rose from 50 to 65-70. Thus, Japan's population is still rising by about 900,000 per year, but the rate of growth is very much less than it was before 1950.[12] The decline in the birth-rate coincided with rising standards of living and more education. The shock of defeat in war, together with the spread of 'western ideas', seems to have hastened the breakdown of old beliefs, and the acceptance of new social customs.

But it would be unwise to reason from these experiences that in due course population growth will slow down and everything will right itself in the less developed countries. In the words of FAO : – 'Europe's demographic revolution is not an inevitable law of nature.'[13] There are several reasons why the course of events could be far less favourable for the poorer countries. The new drugs to combat diseases such as malaria, yellow fever, cholera and typhus are reducing the death-rate much more quickly than birth-control methods are likely to check the birth-rate. Religious objections to birth-control are powerful, and ignorance and fear are formidable obstacles. To many poverty-stricken peasants, large families appear as a source of prestige and a security for old age. The cost of supplying contraceptives and educating people in their use would be prohibitive until cheaper and easier methods are perfected.

Another unfavourable factor is that a majority of people in the less developed countries live under conditions of high population density, and this means that the possibilities of developing large areas of unused land are generally low. This makes it more difficult to break out of 'the circle of poverty', and to achieve the better living conditions in which people may prefer to have smaller families. According to Professor Glass : –

'In the long-term, there must be a re-adjustment of population growth, as well as resources. But new norms of family size cannot develop in a vacuum. And while direct campaigns may well help to spread birth control more quickly than would otherwise be

[12] Ritchie Calder. 'Mathematics of Hunger' (Royal Statistical Society).
[13] FAO. Population & Food Supply, p.9.

the case, the effective establishment of the smaller family requires far more than such campaigns – it requires reinforcement through general social and economic change, which will raise both levels of living and aspirations. A more adequate food supply is an essential requirement here.'[14]

In the short-run, therefore, up to the end of this century, it appears unlikely that population growth will slow down.

This makes all the more urgent the alternative solution, namely to increase food supplies. If, by the year 2000, the earth's population is going to double, reaching 6,000 million people, the world requirement for food is going to be very much higher than at present. To achieve reasonable standards of nutrition in the less developed countries FAO estimate that food production would have to increase by about one third by 1975, and be more than doubled by the end of the century, taking 1958 as the base. In the less developed regions, the increases would have to be much greater, because the present supplies are at a low level.

Size of Future Food Needs[15]

% Increase Required. 1958 equals 100

	1975	2000
Far East	140	245
Near East	143	257
Africa	133	223
Latin America	128	172

Clearly, the targets for these areas are very formidable, 2-2½ times the present level of production.

Is it possible that these targets can be met from the agricultural resources of the earth? This question has been investigated by many experts and scientists with increasing urgency as population projections have risen higher and higher. Professor Dudley Stamp, Director of the World Land-Use Survey, has shown that about three-fifths of the earth's surface are occupied by ice and snow, mountains, deserts and arid regions. Only about two-fifths of the land surface are suitable for human habitation, having physical and climatic conditions permitting the growth of crops

[14] Prof. D. V. Glass 'Hunger Can it be Averted' (British Association).
[15] FAO. Third World Food Survey 1963. Table 27.

needed by man. This 40% of habitable land includes 10% occupied by arable crops and orchards, and about 20% occupied by pastures. In 1959, this provided just over 1 acre in crops and 2 acres in grass per head of the world's population.[16] If the population is going to double in forty years, it is clear that existing farmlands do not provide much margin.

But there is still some habitable land which might be suitable for farming development. According to one estimate, possibly one fifth of the unexploited red soils of Africa and South America might be brought under cultivation, amounting to about 900 million acres, and about another 100 million acres in Sumatra, Borneo, New Guinea, Madagascar and other tropical areas.[17]

FAO consider that:—

'The arid deserts and semi-arid highlands, both in the tropics and the temperate zones, account for another large fraction of the world's uncultivated land. With irrigation, some of these lands could be made highly productive.'[18]

These possibilities exist in Africa, the Near East and many parts of Asia. Equatorial forests and tropical savannahs, which extend on either side of the equator, have low fertility, and are subject to heavy leaching and erosion when cultivated. Settled farming has been successful only in a few favoured spots, as in Java and the Caribbean.[19]

Within the temperate zones, the largest areas of unused agricultural land are in Southern Australia, Brazil and Uruguay. There is also some potential arable land in the northern parts of the USSR and Canada. [20] These temperate lands might be developed relatively quickly, since methods, machines and techniques already in use could be applied. But for the other potential farm land, particularly the tropical savannahs and arid regions, intensive research on suitable methods would be needed and massive

---

[16] Prof. Dudley Stamp. *Our Developing World*, p.37-39.
[17] FAO. Population & Food Supply, p.37.
[18] FAO. *Ibid*, p.37-38. [19] FAO. *Ibid*, p.34-36.
[20] FAO. *Ibid*, p.38.

capital investment on irrigation works, all of which would take a long time.

More speedy increases in food production could be obtained by applying existing knowledge to the lands already in use for agriculture. Better soil management and more use of fertilizers could raise the yield of crops by at least 50%.[21] Further increases could be obtained by control of pests and diseases, which probably destroy up to one quarter of the crops grown.[22] Better methods of breeding and attention to health could enormously raise the productivity of livestock.

In the words of FAO : –

'. . . it is clear that the earth's physical resources and man's technical knowledge are sufficient to multiply the world's production of food many times. But the existence of resources and technical knowledge is not enough in itself to bring about the increase of production which the world desperately needs at present, and the further increases which will be needed in the future to feed the growing population according to a satisfactory standard. To be effective, knowledge must be applied in developing resources and increasing productivity.'[23]

In fact, there are many serious obstacles to the application of improved methods in agriculture. Lack of capital cripples many of the less developed countries. Lack of education tends to make peasant communities suspicious of changes, and means that the supply of well-qualified advisers is inadequate. Lack of fertilizers is possibly the most serious handicap of all in the short run, and without capital and industrial resources, it cannot easily be remedied by the less developed countries. The systems of land tenure in many countries leave the farmer no incentive to increase production, if the greater part of any increase goes to the landlord. The lack of credit facilities, except at exorbitant rates of interest, makes it impossible for farmers to adopt better methods, even if they are aware of them. The economist, Andrew Shonfield, confirms this in a special study of the problems of economic development : –

[21] FAO. *Ibid*, p.39.
[22] Pirie. Food Supplies and Population Growth, p.57.
[23] FAO. *Ibid*, p.41.

'. . . one of the chief barriers to increased food production in Asia is the utterly passive attitude on the part of the mass of the cultivators, the feeling that extra effort cannot be worthwhile, because life is fixed and determined. In the attempt to unravel these attitudes, the FAO, like other observers, soon arrives at the ganglion knot of the village moneylender-trader-boss. . . . People are commonly in debt to him throughout their lives. Yet it would be wrong to imagine that this makes him a simple enemy. The peasants have an ambivalent attitude towards him; he is, after all, the man to whom they can turn in case of need, and he does, after all, provide money on the strength of no more security than a promise to repay it.'[24]

The evidence clearly shows that a technical revolution in farming methods is impossible without social and economic changes, particularly relating to systems of land tenure and credit. In some countries, these changes may take the form of collectivization, as in the Soviet Union and China, with the abolition of private landlords. In others, the provision of co-operative organizations to supply credit, as in Japan, combined with technical advice and supervision, can bring about a big increase in production within the framework of small peasant holdings. Even under the most favourable conditions, a long time is needed to obtain the full results of these changes.

The inescapable conclusion is that there is no quick or easy solution to the vast problem of hunger which afflicts half the human race. Left to themselves, the less developed countries face a grim prospect, as increasing millions are born to starvation and disease. But this is not the inevitable course of human history. One third of mankind is organized in technically advanced industrial societies, with productive systems of agriculture. If their knowledge, technique and resources were brought to bear, the disastrous conditions that threaten humanity need never come about. With massive aid from outside, the less developed countries could break out of the 'circle of poverty', and begin to build up their industry and agriculture. This alternative would require fundamental changes in the economic and financial

[24] Andrew Shonfield. *Attack on World Poverty*, p.123. (Chatto & Windus 1960.)

policies of the advanced countries, in their political relations between one another, and, perhaps most important of all, in their outlook towards their fellow men. For Britain, which is the largest food importer in the world, as well as having close ties with many less developed countries in the Commonwealth, these changes would have far-reaching effects. In the short run, world food shortage could endanger Britain's food supplies. In the long run, if the less developed countries began to emerge from their poverty, Britain could have much to gain from expanding world trade.

CHAPTER II

OUTLINES OF A WORLD FOOD PLAN

HUNGER and malnutrition are today so widespread that nothing less than a united world effort could overcome them. As long ago as 1946, plans for a World Food Board to hold food reserves and stabilize prices were put forward by the newly formed Food and Agriculture Organization. But, as insufficient support was forthcoming, the project had to be dropped.[1] Today, with population growing faster than was expected in 1946, the scale of aid required is correspondingly greater, and the threat of mass starvation is more imminent. The 'Freedom from Hunger Campaign', and the work of Ox-Fam and other voluntary bodies, have begun to awaken public opinion. With some relaxation of tension between the great powers, following the Test Ban Treaty in 1963, there might be some chance of combined action through the United Nations.

Assuming that all the advanced nations decided to co-operate, a World Food Plan could be operated, consisting of three parts:–

   (i)   First Aid for Famines and Emergencies.
  (ii)   Food as Capital Aid.
 (iii)   Investment to raise Agricultural Productivity.

The first objective of a World Food Plan should be to bring effective aid in cases of famine. In recent years, FAO, the Red Cross and individual governments have provided help in many emergencies. Famine may arise from failure of the harvest, as in Kenya in 1961. It can be caused by a typhoon as in Mauritius in 1960, or a hurricane as in the Carribean in 1963, which wrecked

---

[1] Sir John Boyd Orr and David Lubbock. *The White Man's Dilemma.* p.90-96. (Allen & Unwin, 1953.)

much of the sugar cane crop. Famine can also arise from civil war and political upheaval, as in the Congo and Algeria. It would be valuable if there was a permanent emergency service, under FAO, to bring 'first aid' to the people concerned. Stocks of non-perishable foods, such as dried milk, tinned foods and cereals, could be earmarked for this service and stored at convenient points. Governments could be asked to have transport aircraft on call, able to take food, small trucks and personnel to the stricken area. The organization would require a skeleton staff of highly-trained experts, capable of organizing the distribution of food, and co-operating with medical and other relief services. Additional personnel could be recruited locally, or possibly an international volunteer organization could be former, from which suitable people could be drawn for emergencies.

The second objective of a World Food Plan is more long-term, and more ambitious – to use food surpluses from the advanced countries as a form of capital aid to the less developed countries. This has already been started through the World Food Programme, which is to run for three years. Members of the United Nations have been asked to provide food, shipping and other services to aid the less developed countries. This does not mean putting these countries 'on the dole', or handing out charity. The central aim is to help the poorer countries to develop their own industry and agriculture, so that independently they can create a prosperous and civilized life. But there are a number of circumstances in which development cannot even get started due to lack of food. In such cases, food can be the lever which sets in motion the long process of economic growth.

There are occasions when people have been weakened by malnutrition and deficiency diseases, so that they have not the mental or physical energy to raise food production, even if fertilizers, tools and other facilities are available. A supply of protein and vitamin-rich food might be required for few years to build up their strength, so that they could improve their agriculture. In more desperate situations, a supply of grain may be needed to keep people going until the next harvest. Supplies of milk for mothers and babies could create a healthier generation, which will be more likely to accomplish constructive work in the future. In some of the poorer countries, food allowances for students may be indispensable to enable them to get the best out of their education, so that they can reduce the acute shortage of technicians and professional workers. This 'food investment in people' is one of the most important ways of setting going the long process of economic development, since, in the last resort, all development depends upon people.

There are other cases where food supplies act as a form of working capital, whilst a construction project is going on. In a country such as India, if the government receives aid to build a dam or a steel works, many thousands of workers will be taken on locally for the unskilled work. As soon as they receive their wages, they will spend the greater part on food, which they and their families urgently need. But if for technical or social reasons agriculture is at a primitive level, the supplies of extra food will not be forthcoming in the short run, and the effect will be rising prices and inflation. Andrew Schonfield reports that a sample survey in India showed that the average rural worker was unemployed for 140-150 days a year, yet the Government was afraid to institute much-needed public works, because the extra demand for food could not be met.[2] FAO consider that 'international food aid' can be decisive in getting going works of capital construction urgently needed in backward rural areas : –

'Much thought is now being given to the fuller use of under-employed rural manpower for such labor-intensive work as road buildings, rural construction, irrigation etc. Such projects could often be organized on a seasonal basis, avoiding the harvest and other peak periods of agricultural work when with present farming methods the whole rural labor force may be fully extended. In the initial stages of such labor-intensive full-employment policies, good use could be made of the surplus food now available in some developed countries.'[3]

Schemes of this kind are also a way of creating capital for agriculture from within, as opposed to forms of aid coming from the industrial sector or from abroad. As the less developed countries are desperately short of capital, both for new industries and for

[2] Andrew Shonfield. *Attack on World Poverty*, p.170.
[3] FAO. The State of Food and Agriculture 1963, p.133.

agriculture, any methods which make economical use of idle manpower or local resources are obviously of immense value.

The effects of 'international food aid' can go further. Reverting to the big construction jobs like hydro-electric schemes, or industrial plants, the labourers employed on the site will at first spend most of their wages on food. But gradually they will want to spend on other needs, including clothing and simple household goods, and the demand for these would stimulate local textile industries and handicraft workshops. The employees in these trades and independent craftsman would have higher incomes, some of which they would want to spend on food. Thus, from both construction workers and other workers the demand for food would rise, and would begin to stimulate more production in local agriculture. If technical advice was available to the farmers, plus some reforms in the landlord and money-lending system, the long hard struggle to raise productivity would be started. 'International food aid' would be the starting lever to the whole complicated process of economic development, and would be required to span over the period until local agriculture had been made more productive. The large shipments of grain to India from the USA under Public Law 480, which permits the Government to supply surplus food either free or on special terms, have helped India to proceed with her economic plans under pressure of food shortage and growing population.

Yet another way in which food can be used as a form of capital aid is to tide over a rural community for a few years whilst they are improving their agricultural methods. Britain has contributed to such a scheme organized by FAO in North Africa. The object of the scheme is to induce 2,000 nomadic people to settle in one area, by providing food for them and their animals during the season of drought, thus reducing their urge to migrate in search of fodder, and giving them an incentive to introduce grassland management and improved husbandry. Britain sent 13,500 tons of barley in August 1963, and further consignments for two more years, plus the necessary shipping, have been promised as part of the World Food Programme.[4]

The use of food as a form of capital aid is a new conception which can have far greater impact on world hunger than hap-

---

[4] *Farmer and Stockbreeder*, June 18, 1963.

hazard gifts or sporadic offers of surpluses. Examination of the conditions in practically all the less developed countries will reveal many instances where the use of 'international food aid', together with other technical and economic assistance will make possible the 'take-off' from poverty to development. Once a start has been made, economic growth tends to be self-generating, and the aim of all international assistance should be to bring about independent economic development as soon as possible.

The stimulation of economic growth is only the first step towards overcoming the threat of hunger. The third part of a World Food Plan urgently needs to be set in motion at the same time – that is investment in modernizing the whole structure of primitive agriculture. In the early stages, the four most pressing requirements in most of the less developed countries are social reform in the countryside, water supplies, fertilizers and technical advice. It has been shown that industrial development draws a proportion of rural workers off the land, where they are often unemployed for long periods. This may facilitate the reorganization of very small or fragmented holdings. The incentive to produce more must be provided for peasant farmers, by ending exploitation by landlords and moneylenders, either by re-allocation of land, or by co-operative farming, and by the provision of cheap credit facilities.

In many lands, water is by far the most serious limiting factor to farm production. Many governments, with international aid, are carrying out major schemes to harness great rivers to provide electric power and to irrigate large areas of farmland. These schemes include the Aswan High Dam in Egypt, the Volta River Project in Ghana, the Kariba Dam in Central Africa, and the Indus Basin Development Scheme in Pakistan and India. As well as these long-term schemes, some governments are pushing forward small projects for wells and local irrigation schemes, making use of simple equipment and the skill of local craftsmen. This approach is being used in India.

According to FAO: 'Fertilizer use is the spearhead of agricultural development.'[5] It has been estimated that the use of fertilizers could double the output of crops in many of the less developed countries, and thereby bring about the quickest

[5] FAO. The State of Food and Agriculture, 1963, p.13.

increase in food production. But for those countries with no industrial base, it seems that the supply of fertilizers from advanced countries should be treated as a form of immediate capital aid, similar to the supply of food aid. How urgent this is can be demonstrated by the experience in India where it is estimated that increased fertilizer use was responsible for 4.6 million tons of the 11.2 million tons increase in food production during the second five-year plan.[6] High priority should also be given to setting up plant to manufacture fertilizers in the less developed countries, particularly where local materials are available.

Both for works of irrigation and for the erection of fertilizer plants, technical assistance from the advanced countries is essential, especially in the early stages, to supply engineers and surveyors who can draw up plans, to provide heavy equipment, and in some cases to undertake the work on contract. As far as possible, it is better if these schemes depend upon a large enrolment of local labour than on highly mechanized equipment. This absorbs unemployed workers, and stimulates local agriculture and small-scale industry. The scientific resources of the advanced countries are indispensable for research into certain problems which disrupt agriculture in the less developed countries. For example, the Anti-Locust Research Centre in London, financed by the United Nations Organization for Technical Co-operation, has been assisting countries plagued by locusts to tackle the swarms and their breeding grounds with insecticides. The number of swarms of desert locusts found in North Africa has been so much reduced that there is hope that this scourge might be banished permanently. In the same way, research on tsetse fly and foot-and-mouth disease might eventually eradicate these troubles from cattle herds.[7]

Perhaps the most difficult task in technical assistance is to train suitable experts to persuade peasant farmers to try better methods of farming. Experience shows that poverty and hunger give rise to hostility and suspicion towards all outsiders, as well as fostering apathy and superstition. Immense skill and patience is required for such work, in order to win the confidence of the people. Without this approach, the paper plans of government

[6] FAO. *Ibid*, p.144.
[7] *The Guardian*, April 29, 1964.

departments cannot come to life.

In South America, the International Labour Office, with the aid of other UN bodies, has achieved an outstanding success in winning the Andean Indians for development. These people, descendants of the Incas, and numbering some 7 million, have lived for centuries at 8,000-12,000 ft. in the great mountain ranges of Peru, Ecuador and Bolivia. The ILO survey team found that:

'Today, the Andean Indians live in poverty, squalor and ignorance. The old traditional methods of tilling the soil have been lost. Little or no trace remains of the once extremely efficient irrigation systems.'

An ambitious programme was prepared, including schools, health measures, fertilizers and insecticides for agriculture, and training workshops for woodwork and metal work. The whole programme depended upon 'social promoters', local Indians specially trained in the new methods, but living and working in their own communities, where they demonstrated and spread the new ideas. This approach 'from the bottom' seems to have brought remarkable results. According to the report:

'The thirst for education among the Andean Indians seems to be almost insatiable. Schools put up as part of the Programme are packed with pupils the day they open. . . . The Indians themselves do most of the construction work, without thought of pay. In the evenings, after the children have gone home, their places are taken by adults.'

By 1963, the Programme had reached about half a million people, and had won the active support of all three Governments.[8] Given the right approach, and a limited amount of outside help, the Andean Indians responded enthusiastically, and worked together to help themselves.

This brief outline of a World Food Plan shows that in spite of the immensity of the task, the means to overcome world hunger are available. The development of the resources within the poorer

[8] ILO and FAO. 'Hunger and Social Policy', p.58-59.

countries, plus aid from the advanced nations in the form of food, fertilizers, capital equipment and technical assistance, would set going all-round economic growth, as a result of which agriculture could be stimulated and modernized, and levels of nutrition improved. The real problem is not lack of knowledge or lack of means, but lack of *determination* to apply them in practice.

CHAPTER 12

THE AIM OF
EQUALIZATION

WHEN a savage earthquake shattered the Yugoslav city of Skopjie, the immediate and generous response of many nations with constructive help was a moving demonstration of what can be accomplished by united effort. It could be expected that the splendid aim of abolishing world hunger would arouse equal support and enthusiasm. But, in fact, the food situation in the less developed countries has barely regained the inadequate pre-war level, and although their total food production has been rising, the gain has been more than offset by rapidly rising populations. In some countries, standards of nutrition are actually falling. By contrast, in Europe and North America, productivity in agriculture has been rising fast, so that the gap in food supplies per head between the advanced and the less developed nations has been widening. With the rapid rise in world population, the threat of mass starvation is nearer than it was fifteen years ago.

There are a number of reasons why the efforts to solve the world food problem have been ineffective. The majority of states-men pay lip service to the objectives of FAO, but they are not prepared to interfere with their national plans for defence, taxa-tion, free trade and orthodox finance. It comes down to a ques-tion of priorities, and in practice 'freedom from hunger' is relatively low on the list.

During the last fifteen years, the atom bomb and the H bomb have overshadowed world politics, and all the advanced nations have spent vast sums on armaments. Britain and the USSR have been devoting about 7% of their national income to defence, and the USA about 10%. The total annual expenditure on arma-ments by all nations is over £40 billion – 8-9% of the world's output of goods and services. This colossal expenditure is concentrated mainly in the advanced countries – the USA, Canada, the United Kingdom, France, West Germany and the USSR. It is equivalent to two thirds of the entire national income of all the less developed countries combined.[1] It is 1,000 times greater than the present target for the World Food Programme, which is to spread over three years. In comparison with defence budgets, this Programme is a drop in the ocean, which cannot possibly alleviate the hunger of half the human race.

Britain provides many kinds of aid to colonial and independent members of the Commonwealth, as well as to outside countries and to the United Nations. There are many admirable projects on the list which are receiving aid, including the University of East Africa, the Niger Dam, and the Durgapur steel works in West Bengal. But the total sum for all these forms of aid in 1962-63 was £174 million[2] – only one tenth of the £1,700 million spent on defence in that year. Clearly, so long as these immense arms burdens are carried, the prospect of really substantial aid to the developing countries is remote.

Even if disarmament became a reality, and more resources were available for international aid, there would still be serious obstacles to overcoming world hunger. It has been shown that in many less developed countries 'food aid' could be the starting point for economic growth and improved nutrition. But to provide this food on a significant scale would demand very large quantities of grain, meat, powdered milk, dried eggs, cheese and other nutritious foods. It is only within the advanced countries that surpluses of these products could be built up in the near future. Professor Dudley Stamp has emphasized that:–

'. . . from all points of view it is an easier task to increase production from the mid-latitude or temperate lands, where we are familiar with the vagaries of nature, and where we know something of the management of soils and the development of crops than it is to look for immediate development of tropical lands.'[3]

In the short run, the responsibility for raising food production

[1] The United Nations 'The Economic and Social Consequences of Disarmament'.
[2] 'Aid to Developing Countries'. Cmd. 2147. 1963.
[3] Prof. Dudley Stamp. *Our Developing World*, p.178.

rests upon North America, Western Europe and Oceania.

It is sometimes suggested that the proper course is to wait and see what surpluses arise, and then channel them to the countries which are in need. This would be equivalent to using the poorer countries as a kind of dustbin for the convenient disposal of unexpected surpluses. Haphazard and intermittent supplies of this kind would be useless for 'international food aid', which must be planned in advance, regular and sustained, to the point where the receiving country has raised its own economic activity and farm output above the subsistence level. This means that surpluses would have to be produced deliberately, and given away according to a carefully worked out schedule.

It is at this point that serious opposition would arise. Governments would fear that they were making a leap in the dark financially. This fear could be allayed if the contributions of each nation were limited by agreement. At the same time, if defence expenditure was declining, a larger expenditure on 'food aid' would leave taxpayers no worse off. But even more serious would be the fear of excessive surpluses, because farm production cannot be turned on and off like a tap. It takes a long time to get land into good heart, or to build up herds of cattle, sheep and pigs. Once expansion is set going, it is rather like letting the genie out of the lamp in the story of Aladdin : it is not easy to put it back again. At present, much ingenuity and cash is being devoted in the United States to taking land out of cultivation and cutting down the numbers of livestock. In Britain, the Price Review has been used at different times to reduce milk, pig and egg production. In the European Economic Community, there is some fear of excessive supplies of dairy products. Thus, to plan for large and continuing surpluses to be used for 'food aid' would involve the advanced countries and their farmers in some financial risk. There would be the further risk of redundant farming resources in 30-40 years time, if by then the developing countries had built up their own agricultural output. But these risks have to be weighed against the social and political consequences of leaving one half of humanity to suffer from hunger.

Perhaps the most formidable obstacle lies in the economic principles and trading practices which prevent international aid from being effective. The stark fact has to be faced that through unfavourable prices for their exports the developing countries have lost nearly *half* the value of all the grants, loans, and technical assistance which they have received. Most of the less developed countries are exporters of raw materials and food-stuffs, and the trade in these products has grown more slowly than the trade in manufactured goods. This is partly due to the substitution of synthetic materials, such as nylon and artificial rubber, and partly to the rapid growth of agricultural productivity in the industrial countries, combined with protective tariffs. As a result, the prices of primary commodities, other than oil, have risen far more slowly than the prices of industrial goods, in other words, the terms of trade have moved steadily against the developing countries. Between 1950-61, the UN estimate that the terms of trade of primary commodities fell by 26%. Even allowing for the fact that the developing countries export some manufactured articles, and import some primary products, their terms of trade deteriorated by 17%.[4] The UN calculate that : –

'The net inflow of all types of finance (loans, investments and grants-in-aid) from 1950-61 amounted to $47.4 billion (including private reinvestment). This figure drops to $26.5 billion if remittances of interests and profits for the same period are deducted. The fall in the purchasing power of total exports from the developing countries due to the deterioration in the terms of trade has been estimated at about $13.1 billion, which means that after the cost of servicing is deducted, approximately half of the benefit of this inflow was nullified by the adverse effects of the deterioration in the terms of trade.'[5]

The results have been extremely serious in creating an adverse balance of payments for many of the less developed countries, which in turn limits their ability to import essential capital goods or to raise further loans.

The underlying causes of this situation are to be found in the trading principles and practices of the advanced nations. The greater part of world trade is in the hands of the USA, Britain, the Common Market Countries and Japan. All these countries adhere

[4] UN. 'Towards a New Trade Policy for Development', par. 18-19.
[5] UN. *Ibid*, par. 19.

to the theory of free trade. This theory pre-supposes an international division of labour, with each country producing the goods for which it is best adapted, and all countries trading freely without restrictions. But these text-book conditions are far from the realities of the 1960's. In the advanced countries, the workers are organized in trade unions and have secured relatively high standards of living, whereas in the less developed countries the majority of workers are poorly organized, particularly in agriculture, and earn wages which are barely at subsistence level. Production in the advanced countries is increasingly concentrated in the hands of very large combines, corporations and commercial groups, with immense financial power, and often with international connections, whereas in the less developed countries the producers, especially the primary producers of food and raw materials, are scattered and unorganized. As between participants so unequally matched, there cannot possibly be a 'free market' in the classical sense, resulting in a 'fair market price'. Inevitably, the bargaining power of the advanced countries is such that they can dictate terms to the poorer countries, who find themselves paying more for their imports and earning less for their exports. Commenting on the classical theory of free trade, the UN report affirms : –

'The free play concept is admissible in relations between countries that are structurally similar, but not between those whose structures are altogether different as are those of the industrially advanced and the developing countries.'[6]

The tradition of imposing tariffs and excise duties on tropical products, as a convenient means of raising revenue, for example, on tea, coffee and tobacco, has hampered still further the trading efforts of the developing countries. In the opinion of an expert committee of GATT (the General Agreement on Tariffs and Trade), the reduction or abolition of such taxes : – 'could contribute very substantially to raising the export earnings of some of the poorest underdeveloped countries.'[7] Britain has always allowed free entry for products from Commonwealth countries, but there is a tariff

---

[6] UN. *Ibid*, par. 28.
[7] GATT. 'Trends in International Trade', par. 304.

of 9s 4d per cwt. on foreign coffee. In some industrial countries, indirect taxes on tropical products are actually greater than the value of the goods, which obviously discourages consumption. In addition, the granting of concessions for oil, minerals and other natural resources to foreign companies has resulted in a continuing flow of profits and dividends out of the developing countries, particularly where these concessions were obtained under conditions of colonial rule. So, in fact, strong economic forces are tending to widen the gap between rich and poor nations.

The traditional principles of free trade came under heavy fire at the United Nations Conference on Trade and Development in 1964. The group of less developed countries, comprising the majority of the conference, clashed with Britain and other wealthy countries. According to a report in *The Guardian* :–

'They insist on international stabilization devices for food and raw material prices, and for preferential access for their manufactured and semi-manufactured goods at least during their infancy.'[8]

Instead of a free-for-all, the less developed countries want International Commodity Agreements, which would lay down fair prices, sufficient to enable their workers and employers to earn a reasonable living. In Britain, the NFU has been foremost in advocating agreements of this kind, both to help the primary producers, and to ensure our own food supplies. Gradually the conviction has been growing that under conditions of extremely uneven development between different parts of the world, the principles of free trade in reality provide a means for the strong to exploit the weak.

The less developed countries are confronted with similar obstacles in raising loans from the World Bank and other sources. They find that since interest and repayments are on orthodox commercial terms, the burden of servicing and repayment tends to mount until it precludes further expansion. It is estimated that in India, by the end of the third five-year plan in 1966, interest and loan repayments would amount to nearly 35% of the 1960

[8] Karel Norskey. *The Guardian*, April 6, 1964.

export earnings.[9] With only limited prospects of raising staple exports of tea, jute and cotton textiles, this burden would be intolerable, and would make it impossible to raise the additional loans needed for expansion.

To supplement the work of the World Bank, the United Nations in 1959 set up the International Development Association, IDA, under the control of the World Bank, to provide loans on easier terms to countries whose credit would not enable them to borrow on ordinary commercial terms. But the funds allocated to IDA for the first five years were very much less than those available to the World Bank. In the opinion of Andrew Shonfield : –

'The chief element missing in all this is the sense of urgency. What is required now is not so much the slow accumulation of experience on a series of pilot projects, but a political act of will on the part of the rich countries about the quantity of resources they are ready to devote to raising the submerged majority of mankind. As IDA has turned out, it has become the means of enabling the rich to evade the essential problem rather than to solve it.'[10]

Just as free trade prevents the developing countries from earning their way towards prosperity, so orthodox finance prevents them from raising sufficient credit to carry through long-term economic development.

As a consequence of these several obstacles, the twin problems of hunger and poverty are not being solved, and the gap between rich and poor is widening. Humanity is being divided into two groups, whose conditions of life differ so widely that they might almost belong to different planets. This division is bound to create hatred and bitterness, and it might lead to conflicts which could engulf mankind in a nuclear war.

The World Food Congress in Washington in 1963 declared that : 'The persistence of hunger and malnutrition was unacceptable morally and socially.' If this view were adopted, every Government would accept responsibility for increasing world

[9] Andrew Shonfield. *Attack on World Poverty*, p.29-30.
[10] *Ibid*, p.146.

food supplies, just as they accept responsibility for providing hospitals for the sick in their own country, or schools for the children. The equalization of conditions between nations would receive high priority, and ways and means would be found of adjusting agricultural, trading and financial policies accordingly. The first and hardest step is to win conviction that world hunger can no longer be tolerated.

This conviction could be reinforced by the economic benefits which would eventually follow the process of equalization. Reference has already been made to the struggle for markets between industrial countries – the restless and uneasy competition, in which first one country and then another faces a balance of payments crisis. It would seem logical that if world trade could expand step by step with expansion of production in the various countries, there would be more opportunity for all. In fact, this has not happened. Between 1920-57, it is estimated that in the non-Communist world production of commodities has increased by 100%, but exports have increased by only about 50%.[11] The greatest barrier to trade expansion is the extreme poverty of one half of the human race, with the result that they cannot enter into trading relations with the rest of the world, either as buyers or sellers. The majority of these people are engaged in agriculture. Lord Boyd Orr has pointed out that if their income could be raised, even by £10 or £20 per annum, this would provide an immense increase in the demand for consumer goods, which would stimulate economic activity. Once the developing countries reach the point of self-sustaining economic growth, they would provide an almost unlimited demand for manufactured goods of all kinds from the industrial countries. So it follows that the advanced countries have everything to gain in the future by diverting resources now to overcome the problems of poverty and hunger.

[11] GATT. 'Trends in International Trade', par. 81.

CHAPTER 13

THE IMPLICATIONS FOR BRITAIN

THE 'population explosion' and the menace of world hunger have far-reaching implications for Britain, more so than for almost any other advanced nation. For countries which are self-supporting in food supplies, the issue is mainly one of social and moral obligation towards their fellow men. For Britain, it is much more complicated. First and foremost, our food supplies are especially vulnerable, since nearly half our total requirements are imported. Any major change in the supply or price of food on the world markets could seriously affect our standard of living, and our balance of payments. As the centre of the Commonwealth, Britain has many long-standing obligations both to those who export food to us and to those who need aid to lift themselves out of poverty. So far as farming resources are concerned, Britain is well endowed, and has a big potential for expansion. This imposes some responsibility for helping to raise world food supplies. It is not easy to weigh up all these requirements and obligations, and to arrive at an accurate assessment.

There are several courses which the Government could follow in relation to the problem of world hunger. It is sometimes suggested that Britain should cut down on agriculture, concentrate on industrial production, and import food from the undeveloped countries, thus providing them with a good market. But while this approach is possible for tropical products, the less developed countries in Africa, Asia and the Middle East cannot supply us with meat, grain, dairy products and other temperate foodstuffs. The most practical way to help these countries is to continue the policy of free entry for their products, and to pay fair prices for them.

Some economists contend that there will not be a world food shortage. They would agree that in terms of *human need*, there is an acute shortage of food, and as populations increase, it is likely to get worse, but they argue that as the starving people cannot afford to buy food, their needs do not constitute an *effective demand*, and will not influence world food supplies. Mr Gavin McCrone writes:–

'But even in the event of population outstripping the growth in food production, there is little likelihood of the Far East becoming an importer of food on a large scale. The harsh fact remains that apart from what can be obtained from loans and grants, the ability to import is limited by the ability to pay. . . . Therefore, even in the worst case, where population were to run ahead of food supplies, there would be no call on the food supplies of the rest of the world, apart from that of charity, and the population would sink back to its old position of limiting itself by famine and disease.'[1]

This cold-blooded outlook consigns large sections of humanity to 'famine and disease'. If this is the end result of applying the principles of laissez-faire economics, it is surely time a new set of economic principles were adopted.

The third alternative is to accept that the raising of conditions in the less developed countries is urgently necessary, socially, morally and economically, and that it is within our power to do it. Just as slavery, which was once widespread, is today condemned and rejected by every nation, so too mass starvation and poverty will not be tolerated, once men and women are convinced that they can be overcome.

When the process of equalization begins, it will make economically effective a vast unsatisfied demand for food, particularly in the period before the more backward systems of agriculture have been modernized. A number of developing countries, whilst struggling to improve their own agriculture, are likely to become buyers on the world market for staple foods. Some experts believe that India will need to import food in large quantities as industrialization proceeds, because due to religious taboos the improvement in farming practices is likely to be very slow. In

[1] Gavin McCrone. *Economics of Subsidising British Agriculture*, p.163. (Allen & Unwin. 1962.)

1961-62, China, which is undertaking rapid industrialization, as well as re-organizing the peasants into communes, suffered two exceedingly bad harvests, and faced a serious food shortage. Their economy had developed to a point where they could afford to buy on the world market, and they purchased 4½ million tons of wheat and barley from Canada, at a cost of £130 million. The world stock of wheat at that time was about 46 million tons, of which Canada held 13 million. Thus, this one transaction was equal to nearly one third of Canada's stock at the time, and nearly 10% of the world stock. This was followed by a crop failure in 1963 in the 'virgin lands' in Siberia in the USSR. Here, in spite of great progress in mechanizing agriculture, the supply of food was inadequate to provide the standard of living demanded by the rapidly growing urban population, and the Soviet Union negotiated with the USA and Canada to purchase 4·5 million tons of wheat.[2]

In Europe, particularly in France and Italy, there is a shortage of beef. In the first six months of 1964, French buyers were operating in British markets, and there has been more competition for Argentine beef. Japan is also beginning to buy lamb from New Zealand. These examples indicate what is likely to happen if a number of other countries begin to develop industrially and financially to a point where they can purchase food on the world market to supplement deficiencies in local supplies, and to offset natural calamities. These new buyers are beginning to influence the international markets in food.

World trade in food consists of two parts – temperate and tropical. The exporters of temperate foodstuffs are relatively few in number, and all of them are industrialized or semi-industrialized countries – the United States, Canada, Australia, New Zealand, the Argentine, Holland, France and Denmark. In varying degrees, all these countries make use of modern scientific methods. Those in Europe have very little unused agricultural land on which they could expand production. In Canada, Australia and the Argentine, there are some additional lands which could be used, but they are rather less favourable in climate and accessibility than those already being farmed. Only in the United States, where land is being taken out of cultivation, is there likely to be a reserve of good land with favourable

[2] FAO. *Production Year Book.* 1962-63.

climate. Outside the United States, production of temperate foodstuffs on new lands would probably be more costly than existing supplies.

But all these countries could raise output on their present farmlands by intensifying production and improving efficiency by higher yields of grain, better grassland management and improved livestock husbandry. As the current standards are advanced, increases in production could not be expected overnight. In the short run, therefore, with more buyers competing for supplies, there is likely to be some rise in the price of temperate foodstuffs. Further, if through a World Food Plan grain, meat, and dairy products were produced on contract as a form of capital aid to developing countries, this would also increase the pressure on supplies.

So far as tropical foods are concerned, rice is of decisive importance as a staple food in many parts of the Far East, the largest producers being China, India, Pakistan, Japan, Indonesia, Burma and Thailand. The supply of rice does not directly affect Britain, but there could be an indirect effect if rice-eating people became accustomed to wheat and began to purchase grain on the world market.

For Britain, the most important tropical foods are cane sugar, tea and oil seeds, for making margarine, followed by cocoa and coffee. Supplies of these products, other than coffee, are drawn mainly from Commonwealth countries – the West Indies, India, Pakistan, Ceylon, Nigeria and other African countries. Supplies of these products are adequate at present, and in some cases in excess of demand. On strictly economic grounds, there is less likelihood of immediate price rises. But towards these countries Britain has special obligations as developing members of the Commonwealth. To help these countries increase their foreign earnings, Britain should support measures to remove taxes from tropical products and to set up International Commodity Agreements which would stabilize the prices of these items. If the rural workers producing tropical foods began to press for higher incomes, prices might be raised, particularly if other developing countries began to buy more of these products. So it appears likely that for the time being the supply of tropical products will be plentiful and prices will remain stable, but in the more distant future, as part of the effort to raise living standards in rural communities, the prices might be increased.

This, then, is the probable balance sheet on food supplies for Britain in the event of a comprehensive World Food Plan being carried out – additional competition for temperate foodstuffs, with some rise in prices; adequate supplies of tropical products, but with political and social pressure to pay more for them. Throughout all the developing countries, food is likely to be scarce for several decades, whilst primitive agriculture is being modernized. As purchases on the international market increase, it is reasonable to conclude that there will be a world food shortage. The severity of the shortage will depend on how quickly and how successfully food production in all countries can be raised.

The possibility of a world food shortage should arouse serious concern in Britain. It will be recalled that due to our own rising population and higher standards of living, we shall need at least 30-40% more food by the year 2000. It would surely be wise to study the problem in good time, and make plans accordingly, rather than to bury our heads in the sand.

If a more detailed survey of world trends confirmed these conclusions, the first and most urgent step would be to prevent the destruction of farming resources in the United Kingdom. The greatest threat to our farming potential is the reckless seizure of fertile farmland for housing, motorways, new towns and airfields. These developments are essential to a thriving industrial nation, but Britain cannot afford to lose the limited and priceless heritage of good arable land, on which 2-3 tons per acre of grain can be grown, or 14 tons of potatoes. Since the war, farmland has been taken over at the rate of about 38,000 acres per year.[3] If population increased by 18-20 millions by the end of the century, another 6-7 million homes would be needed, assuming rather less than three persons per family. At the moment, new house building is at the rate of about 10 families per acre, on the average, so that 6-7 million additional families would require up to 600-700,000 acres, plus nearly as much again for industry, commerce, schools, shopping centres and parks, making a total of up to 1½ million acres. To this must be added airfields, motorways, reser-

[3] Dr Robin Best. 'Land for New Towns' (Town and Country Planning Association).

voirs, brickfields, gravel pits and other miscellaneous land occupiers. All in all, between 1 million and 2 million acres could be lost from the 31 million acres of crops and grass in the United Kingdom, in a period in which there is likely to be an increase of 30-40% in the demand for food.

These few facts indicate that land resources will need to be used with the utmost care, according to a well worked out land budget, in which agriculture should be given a high priority. The establishment of a Ministry of Land and Natural Resources is encouraging, always providing it is not treated as one of the 'poor relations' of government. Land of the highest fertility for crops and horticulture should be exempted entirely from building. New development should be steered to the less productive lands, including the sandy heaths and the thin chalklands, which cannot produce as much food. If the very best land, particularly in the eastern half of Scotland and England, were safeguarded, then with rising yields of crops, it would be possible to offset to some extent the loss of other farm land.

The central areas of many cities have become twilight areas of slums, old workshops, yards and railway sidings. Many of these districts could be redeveloped comprehensively, to house the people in a mixture of houses and flats, with gardens and trees between, to the great benefit of city workers. Though very expensive at first, this would be a more truly economical solution than extending suburbs endlessly into irreplaceable farmland. In heavily congested areas of tenements and back-to-back houses, it may not be possible to rehouse all the people on the same site. If new towns are required, they should be built on land of low agricultural value, and in parts of the country which are declining in population and deficient in industrial growth. By promoting a better balance between all areas of the United Kingdom, a more economical use could be made of manpower and transport facilities, and the generations to come would have a more attractive environment to live in.

As well as preserving our most productive farmlands, plans should be considered to stimulate better use of the 17 million acres of hill land and rough grazings. As the price of lowland farms rises higher and higher, the cost of improving and reclaiming hill pastures will become more competitive, and with the rising demand for meat it will become an economic proposition to invest more in buildings, services and amenities on hill farms. These lands could increase the breeding herds of cattle and sheep, and make possible the larger supply of meat which will be needed. They could also accommodate great areas of forest, which would provide additional jobs and reduce our reliance upon imported timber. As these developments are bound to take a long time, the sooner they are begun the better.

The planning of land use requires urgently to be co-ordinated with the planning of water resources. The growth of population and industry is constantly raising the demand for water, and ironically in some areas of this rain-soaked island water is becoming scarce. This is true in parts of East Anglia and in some of the great cities, such as Manchester. Farmers, too, are using more water with the installation of irrigation systems. Water engineers are demanding huge areas of farmland to build new reservoirs. In Buckinghamshire, for example, seventy farms are threatened with inundation. Yet other experts suggest that several really comprehensive schemes, such as damming the Wash or the Solway Firth, would conserve far greater quantities of water, and at the same time provide electric power and reclaimed farmland. Our Dutch neighbours have pioneered schemes of this kind time and again with outstanding success, and with great benefit to their economy. But in Britain there is a serious danger that long-term and radical schemes will be shelved in favour of ad hoc makeshifts, which will neither preserve our farming resources nor solve the water shortage.

Next to the land itself, the skilled farming labour force is the asset which is wasting away most rapidly. The low wages of agricultural workers, relative to other industries, has led to a steady loss of workers at the rate of about 25,000 per year. All too often it is the highly skilled men, with years of experience behind them in handling complex machinery and valuable live-stock, who become embittered by the inadequate pay and prospects, and decide to emigrate or to move into industry. These men cannot be replaced overnight by young recruits or students just out of Farm Institute. The income squeeze on farmers is also driving out some men and women of ability who occupy small and medium farms, and who cannot achieve a fair living due to lack of capital. Whilst there are inevitably some farm units which are too small, or too unfavourable in location to be economically viable, and which must sooner or later be amalgamated with larger holdings, it does not necessarily follow that the more farmers who get out the better. It depends how much food is needed from British agriculture, and some clear decision should be reached, before high quality manpower has been too heavily depleted.

Modernization of farms is a complex process, including new buildings and layouts, the breeding up of livestock, systems of cropping, the training of workers, and the evolution of management. These combined resources take many years to assemble and to organize to a high level of efficiency. At present, the industry requires many measures to improve its performance, particularly better management advice and training, enlarged veterinary services and more rapid replacement of old buildings. Re-organized marketing systems and more extensive credit facilities are also urgently needed to enable farmers to plan and carry through their work successfully. These changes need to go on steadily, with a fair measure of security on prices and incomes. But the twin pressures of rising costs and frozen incomes, which have been imposed on farmers in recent years, are bound to hinder the long process of modernization, and may even bring it to a halt. In the face of a world food shortage, a standstill on farm improvement would be disastrous. Whatever decision is finally taken about the total production required from British agriculture, the immediate policies of the Government should give farmers both the confidence and the incentive to stay in business and go on raising productivity.

CHAPTER 14

THE CASE FOR EXPANSION

THE subject of Britain's food supplies is so vast that only a bare outline can be given in a book of this scope. But from the facts which have been assembled there emerge clearly certain broad conclusions, which may provoke further research and discussion.

Perhaps the most important conclusion is that so far as Britain is concerned, the nineteenth century is over. The United Kingdom is no longer 'the workshop of the world', and there is no new Canadian west waiting to be opened up to provide us with unlimited supplies of cheap food. The struggle for industrial markets is intense, and strictly limits the amount of food we can afford to buy from abroad. As overseas supplies become more expensive, and as our agriculture becomes more competitive, the balance of economic advantage is shifting towards greater production of food from our own resources.

The 'population explosion' is creating a crisis in food supplies in many parts of the world, and the estimates of FAO suggest that in the next twenty or thirty years the pressure of population may outstrip food production in many of the less developed countries, leading to mass hunger and famine. This terrible threat could be averted by concerted action on a large scale by the advanced countries, and there are compelling reasons, moral, social and economic, for carrying out a comprehensive World Food Plan. The effect of this in the short run would be to raise substantially the demands upon existing world food supplies, during the period in which primitive agricultural systems were being modernized. It is probable that the food shortage would get worse before it gets better.

There are several unknown factors which could modify this forecast. The USA has enormous agricultural resources, which have been used to help some of the less developed countries, and these could be expanded. It would create difficult problems if the

USA attempted to supply the needs of advanced countries like Britain, because their traditional policies of very high tariff protection would make it extremely difficult to pay for the food imports. Dollar indebtedness could lead to the sale of more British firms and assets to American interests, with a loss of independence. Another uncertain factor is the agricultural potential of the Soviet Union. Hitherto, Soviet farming has had to take second place to industrial development, but if more capital and managerial talent were diverted to agriculture, output might rise very rapidly, and the Soviet Union would revert to being a net exporter of food. In China, too, there are many signs that the Communist Revolution is releasing the traditional skill and ingenuity of the peasants, and long before full mechanization is possible, they may raise food production very significantly by flood control and irrigation, and by better methods of cultivation. Developments of this kind would improve the world food situation, but would not remove the danger of starvation in other areas. Even on the most optimistic forecasts, food is likely to be scarce and prices on the world markets are likely to rise.

It is this which makes Britain so vulnerable, particularly as regards temperate foodstuffs. Our own population is growing, and by the end of the century, there may be an additional 20 million people to feed. To provide everyone with a full and healthy diet will require a lot more food. At the moment, farm output is expanding, and is meeting the needs of our growing population, with a bit to spare. In these conditions, to slash farm production, or to treat our farmlands as merely a place to take the dog for a walk, would seem to be irresponsible lunacy. Further, to destroy some of the world's most fertile farmland under a flood of new towns, in which twenty-five years hence there may be plenty of motor cars, but not enough food, is a planner's nightmare. Whatever else cannot be accomplished, the food supply of the British Isles must be safeguarded, and in the conditions of the 1960's this means that farm expansion should continue.

It is not possible without more detailed study to determine how fast and how far this expansion should go. The more cautious would be content with 75-80% self-sufficiency in temperate foodstuffs, while the more ambitious would opt for 90-100%, with a much bigger export trade in food and farm products. What is most needed is the recognition that our farming resources are one of Britain's greatest national assets, and that we have an immense farming potential which can be used to ensure an adequate food supply in the future. It can also contribute substantially to the growth of the economy and the balance of payments. The technical revolution in farming methods, which is taking place in many advanced countries, is proceeding exceptionally fast in Britain, and is gradually making our costs more favourable in comparison with those of overseas suppliers. This will steadily reduce the need for price subsidies.

But farmers and farmworkers are human beings, with feelings and aspirations similar to those of their fellow citizens. Within an affluent society they are embittered to find that their incomes are lagging so far behind, in spite of all their hard work and their intensive efforts to raise productivity. Farming expansion depends upon people, and their co-operation will not be forthcoming if they do not feel they are receiving a fair deal.

Over many parts of the countryside there stride mighty electric pylons, carrying power to homes, factories and farms. These pylons are a symbol of better living conditions and economic progress. Behind them lies the scientific and technical ability which is putting Britain in the front rank of nations generating electricity from atomic energy. Is it too much to hope that British people will come to recognize that the plough, like the pylon, is a symbol of productive effort and scientific knowledge, essential to the continued life of these islands?

INDEX

INDEX

For Product Safety Concerns and Information please contact our EU
representative GPSR@taylorandfrancis.com Taylor & Francis Verlag GmbH,
Kaufingerstraße 24, 80331 München, Germany

Printed and bound by CPI Group (UK) Ltd, Croydon, CR0 4YY
08/05/2025
01864377-0001